Dear Brian,

Thank you for all you do for writers / authors! May all your doors shall Good & special surprises! Best always,

Enjoy!

~ Sande 6-13-15

Best Wishes! Sandra J. Cropsey

"~ Sande"

Who's There?

Sandra Jones Cropsey

Outskirts Press, Inc.
Denver, Colorado

Who's There?
A Humorous Spiritual Journey In The Southern Crescent

Cover design by Carol Wubbena

Outskirts Press, Inc.
http://www.outskirtspress.com

ISBN: 978-1-4327-0197-0

Outskirts Press and the "OP" logo are trademarks belonging to Outskirts Press, Inc.

PRINTED IN THE UNITED STATES OF AMERICA

Dedicated

to

the three men in my life—

Paul, Justin, and Brad.

Cover Artist Biography

Artists always put a twist on eccentricity. . . and the unknown becomes the artistic challenge. You won't find her behind the green door, but artist and poet Carol Wubbena peers behind the portals of history for creative inspiration. You will find the artist, whose painting name is Cara, amongst the massive columns and stacks of books of a restored 1910 Carnegie Library. Ironically, the library is her own. Her studio in the Georgian Revival building, is located in Barnesville, Georgia; far away from the excitement of the archaeological excavations that inspire her vibrant symbolic paintings and performances. The uniquely elegant and sometimes curious décor of her living area garnered media attention from HGTV and *Southern Living Magazine*. Her paintings have been featured on Georgia Public Broadcasting and can be seen at www.carastudios.com.

Acknowledgment

Special thank you. . .

. . .to my editor, Joyce Durham Barrett, "Joy" to those of us who love her. A beautiful person, Joy is kind and good and gentle, a shining example of Christ's love. Thank you for your encouragement, your inspired help, and most of all for your friendship. My life is richer knowing you.

Prefix

"Behold I stand at the door, and knock. . ."

—Revelations 3:20

Chapter 1

You Can Call Me Sister

Seemed harmless at first for Momma to keep Bunk's amputated leg in the freezer. The leg was no longer of any use to Bunk, and it helped Momma with the fact that Bunk, as she knew him, was gone. Ivylee and I had called our daddy "Bunk" since childhood, and to us, doing so was as natural as saying "y'all." When our Bunk lost his leg, he also lost his ability to reason and started acting so peculiar that Momma banned him from the house. He lived outside much like a family pet, and we all called him "Precious."

"Precious, baby, what are you doing out there in that pond?" Momma yelled at least once a day during those humid days of summer.

"You not baptizing Miss Leila's cat again, are you? Remember, we don't baptize every day. Makes it common to do a thing every day. Now you be careful you don't fall and bump that noggin of yours." Momma kept a watchful eye on Precious and followed him around much like a

1

young mother toddling after a two-year-old.

At the beginning of my third year at the state university, where I had decided to study forestry, I received the call to come home and "run the farm." According to Momma, Bunk had gone berserk on her. Frantic as though she were calling from the midst of a war zone, Momma was beside herself with worry and fear.

"Sister, come home. I need you. Ivylee's sick with fever and has been delirious for days, and Bunk's in the hospital. Had an accident with his hunting gun, and his mind has done slipped into reverse."

Momma couldn't run the farm and tend to these two at the same time. When I arrived home, I found Momma so confused and detached that I had to put her to bed for several days, until she could get her wits about her enough to function. When we moved forward with our lives later that fall, we found ourselves wedged into a reality that neither Momma nor I could grasp, let alone justify. Having always been a person with a pleasant attitude, Momma hid her pain from the world *and* from herself. Her worried heart was torn with despair, and she patched those tears with a duct tape of make believe.

Make believe was what made Bunk "Precious," but before he became "Precious," he was just Bunk, and before he became "Precious/Bunk," he was the son of a jackleg circuit preacher by the name of Oleander Lowry.

Momma and Bunk married when she was only fourteen. "I was outside playing in my playhouse the day Bunk first came to call on me. Making pretend fried chicken legs out of mud and sticks and collards and fatback out of hedge leaves and rocks. Why, I barely knew how to cook anything besides mud pies. And your Meemaw, she always said I had an imagination that could carry me to Timbuktu and back, and it did."

Sometimes, I wondered if in her mind Momma was still that young girl. Other than these little snippets of memories, she never talked much about that time in her life.

Momma's family was dirt poor and didn't even own the dirt. Like chickens in a barnyard, they could hardly scratch out enough to get by. Her parents were sharecroppers, who shared, worked and lived in a small shack on a chicken farm that belonged to somebody else. Times were so hard Momma's family could no longer afford to feed her, so they took care of their baby girl as best they could, by marrying her off at the tender age of fourteen. Still a child, what Momma brought with her to the marriage was an extraordinary ability when it came to make believe, and when Bunk lost his leg, this ability came to true light. What may have been a flickering candle of fantasy in her past became a fully lit kerosene lantern in our present.

At the beginning of Bunk's mishap, with the exception of the wanderings and the confusion, all seemed innocuous, but then one night, Bunk built a fire in the living room, which wouldn't have been so bad, except we don't have a fireplace. The event so alarmed Momma that she moved Bunk to the tool shed the following week. After that incident, Bunk's only manifestation inside the house came in the form of his leg.

Before going berserk on Momma, Bunk mostly spoke when spoken to. "How come Bunk doesn't talk much, Momma," Ivylee asked once while we were helping Momma prepare her applesauce cakes for Christmas.

"Bunk's what you might call a thinking man, Honey, and I don't reckon them kind say a lot. He always said what most people had to say would have been better left unsaid and wasn't worth the air it arrived on. Didn't take long for me to learn that Bunk's actions were his way of saying 'I love you.'" Whenever Momma spoke of Bunk, her voice would sound soft and tender, as though wrapped in some satin memory.

Not to be outdone that day, Ivylee declared while chopping pecans, "Well, my Mr. Robinson just showers me with his endless proclamations of love each and every day. Some days I just get downright weary listening to it."

Momma smiled as she continued stirring the batter for the applesauce cakes. When she did not respond, Ivylee added, "He even writes it across the sky."

"In invisible ink no doubt, just like him." I scooped up a handful of pecan halves to reserve for decorating the caramel icing on the cake.

"I'll have you know my Mr. Robinson is a man of character."

"Who doesn't exist."

"Now, girls," Momma chided. "Let's not finish the day with prickly words. We never know who might not see the light of dawn tomorrow, and, God forbid, when that happens, what you're left with is this swollen conscience just bursting at the seams. And we don't want that, do we?"

Such was the gist of most of our conversations. Ivylee and I had never stopped competing with one another, although I'm not sure what we were competing for. Her Mr. Robinson was a figment of her imagination, someone she created to fill the void between her ears, as well as the one in her bed.

After Bunk's lapse into dementia, he talked more, although nothing he said made much sense. And even though Bunk talked, it was to people who weren't there, and those of us who were, may as well not have been. But after Momma moved Bunk to the tool shed, he stopped talking altogether for a while. When he did talk again, which was seldom, Bunk only talked to Momma. Whatever he had to say went unsaid, and the air his words would have arrived on became still and stagnant.

I cannot recall the first time I realized my family was different. Maybe I had been born with this awareness. Whenever it was pointed out to me, I never argued the fact, knowing fully well that to do so would be like arguing that the earth was flat. And even if from where you're standing the earth appears flat, in the very heart of your mind, you know it's round and can be proven at any moment. I knew my family was different, and I didn't have to open my eyes or my ears to know that.

Even though Momma's life had been far from easy, the harshness of it never showed in either her outlook or her youthful complexion. A petite woman, Momma's plumpness seemed to round out all the sharp edges of unpleasantness life passed along. Always soft-spoken with a heart capable of being moved by almost any circumstance, Momma met the challenges in her life with childlike simplicity.

Bunk was ten years older than Momma. Pensive-looking, he gave the impression that something was set in him, something just beneath the surface that had never been allowed to bud. A man who could direct a hog killing in the fall and hold a butterfly in the spring, Bunk was always at ease.

Although we knew only bits and pieces about Bunk's daddy, we had been told he was a "preacher man," a circuit preacher who was staunch and intolerant in his beliefs. In the early days of our childhood, when Bunk spoke of him, his voice would take on an air of reverence and awe. While Bunk whittled some small critter for mine and Ivylee's pretend zoo, he often called the image of his circuit rider father to mind.

"Oh, he's a preacher, girls, a big man who commands

respect. A man of God, who travels all over delivering The Word to the unbelievers. God bless him, your grandpa has saved many a soul from damnation, that's for sure, and I'd say they's probably no greater calling in life than that."

While Momma hung wet clothes on the clothesline, Bunk would sit on an old tree stump in the back yard, whittle away at some piece of soft wood, and share memories of his Papa. I don't recall Momma ever saying much during these times.

"Sister, hand me that clothespin."

"Yes, Momma." Like us, Momma just listened, and so I assumed she was as awed by Bunk's father as he was.

"Momma? You want me to hand you another pair of overalls? Momma?" When I looked up at her, she looked far away. I thought maybe she saw somebody coming toward us, and so I looked where she looked, but didn't see anybody. "Momma? What's wrong?"

"Must have gotten something in my eye." She wiped her apron across her eyes, placed her finger to her lips to shush me and pointed for me to hand her another clothespin.

Later, when we were washing the supper dishes, I asked her why she was crying.

"Sometimes us women folk just have to cry, Honey."

Like Momma, Bunk was short and plump. The two of them were like a pair of roly-poly salt and peppershakers in both shape and demeanor. While Momma added an enhanced, although sort of off-the-wall, flavor to life, Bunk in recent years had become dark and elusive, a peppercorn unable to provide any pungency to his life's purpose.

Neither Ivylee nor I looked like either Momma or Bunk, and as a result, it would have required little effort to convince either of us that we had been adopted.

"Ivylee have you ever noticed that neither of us look

like either Momma or Bunk?"

"Momma says I'm tall and willowy like her Aunt Louisa. I could have probably been a model, that is, if I weren't so shy."

"Shy? The only time you might ever be shy, Ivylee, is when you're sleeping, and the only thing you could model with that pasty-white complexion is institutional wear, but you could model a bed since you're in it most of the time. If you'd get outside once in a while, you wouldn't have that sickly pallor to your skin."

While I have never doubted Ivylee's frailty, I also have never believed that frailty was as weak and delicate as she would have Momma believe. To my way of thinking, Ivylee's mind was already weak prior to her illness, and the illness only illuminated that fact, sort of like a neon sign that suddenly, seemingly out of nowhere, appears in the dark.

"You know I'm not well, Sister."

"If your illness left you with any disability, Ivylee, it was that of laziness, a condition you have yet to overcome."

"Well, at least I'm not as plain as a bowl of oatmeal."

"No, your oatmeal is between your ears."

Ivylee stuck out her tongue at me, which is how most of our conversations ended. But she was right. I am plain, as plain and boring as a one-a-day vitamin, and running this farm has only heightened my plainness. While I am only four years older than Ivylee, most of the time, I look fourteen years older. The stress of maintaining the farm and surviving my lot in life shows its signs in all my facial features—the darkness around my eyes, the lines across my brow, the creases that flare out from each side of my nose. I have reached middle age ahead of schedule, and when I look into the mirror, which is seldom, all I see is what never was. My resentment for my life's situation has turned to bitterness, a daily dose of disappointment I am obligated to swallow. As a result, I often lash out with snide, and sometimes unkind, remarks and criticisms. I also believe I lash out at times to entertain myself and to try to hang on to, with white knuckles if necessary, what little sanity I still possess, given my circumstances. Most of my lashing out usually lands in Ivylee's direction, not just because she makes for a convenient target, but also because she is so annoying.

"Ivylee, hibernation is not supposed to be a constant state. Even bears come out eventually. . .If you get any lazier, Ivylee, Momma's gonna have to hire somebody to breathe for you." Ivylee ignored me most of the time and became quite adept at doing so.

Our family life centered and simmered in our living room. A three-seater sofa and an overstuffed chair, a favorite roosting place for Ivylee, filled most of the room. A coat rack made by my great grandfather stood to one side of the door next to a lace-curtained window. On the other side of the door sat an old stove that had stopped working years before and was to have been hauled off, but had only made it as far as the front door. The stove became of special significance to Ivylee, her "poetica performance stage," her "p.p.s.," which for me, stood for perfectly putrid stuff.

A cherry-stained sideboard sat against the wall between the coat closet and the hall door that led to the kitchen and bedrooms. Handmade oak end tables anchored each end of the sofa, and although the coffee table could not lay claim to any coffee-table books, it did hold Momma's Bible when not in use. For Momma, her Bible was her Owner's Manual, a watering hole where she refreshed her spirit, whether she happened to understand it or not. Our coffee table was a small coffin, within which Bunk's leg lay at rest during memorial services.

"Okay, girls, let's get the living room ready. Ivylee, help your sister place the coffee table on top of the sideboard. I'll go get Bunk's leg outta the freezer. Sister, would you arrange the flowers?"

Momma purchased the coffin the same week she moved Bunk to the tool shed. All she had left of Bunk was his leg, and she held onto that leg as though it were her last and only hope.

"Oh, my poor Bunk." Momma leaned forward, stroked the coffin and sighed at least once a day as though the coffin were some pitiful, abandoned baby for whom she had been assigned the task of caretaker by an eminent, all-knowing, celestial presence.

"Why, Bunk will be back any day now to collect his leg, don't you think?" Most times, the question went unanswered and had become little more than a routine reassurance she repeated to herself.

For Momma, this preoccupation with Bunk's leg had become a huge, hungry hog she felt compelled to feed on a regular basis, and that was about the only thing in our household that was "regular." As hard as she tried, Momma just could not feed that hog enough, and initial once-a-week memorial services soon became once-a-day memorial services.

Every day we gathered at Momma's appointed time and carried on like misfit mourners in a circus freak show over Bunk's sad-looking, shriveled-up leg.

"Okay, girls, let's gather 'round. Who wants to be on the program today?"

My dimwit sister, Ivylee, strung weird words together into arrangements she called poetry and recited that nonsense from atop that old stove in the living room while

Momma hummed hymns in the background. In the daily devotion of makeshift services, Momma would glorify, eulogize, and memorialize Bunk's leg. As certain as the clock that had stalled in time on our living room stove, Momma prayed over it, sang over it, and generally carried on over that leg like she thought the thing Lazarus about to rise from the dead.

For the length and breadth of these services, Momma would routinely have the leg dressed up for every kind of holiday imaginable. On Valentine's Day, Bunk's leg sat in the center of a red, papier-mâché heart surrounded by whatever valentines were popular that year. For Easter, the leg was dressed in a chocolate-brown bunny suit with an odd-shaped carrot sewn on the front, a fuzzy, white cottontail attached to the back, and large pink ears. For the fourth of July, the leg sported a red, white and blue turban with a small U.S. flag sticking out the top. Labor Day's get-up was a straw hat and overalls embroidered with a small shovel. The color for Christmas was bright red, and the costume was made of crushed velvet with white, faux fur trim.

My personal favorite by far was Halloween, without a doubt, a holiday made for this family *and* for Bunk's leg. Propped up in the center of our sofa was an orange pumpkin made with luminescent fabric that shimmered and glowed in the dark and onto which jagged triangular eyes and a crooked smile had been appliquéd, and inside that outfit was Bunk's leg. The effect of seeing my daddy's leg sitting in the center of the sofa dressed as a glow-in-the-dark pumpkin is not an image to be taken to the grave, but one that surely belongs there.

"My, but doesn't he look just darling? I do believe he looks more charming this year than last. What do you think, girls?"

Most often, Ivylee would mimic some response she thought Momma wanted to hear, and I generally ignored the two of them, but not because I am a deep-thinker. Some things are just better left not thought about.

In the beginning, the services were primarily spiritual, and for Momma, they remained spiritual, but in terms of my own participation, I had begun to deliver sermons related to some nature television show I had recently seen on public broadcasting or from some article I had read in a nature magazine. One of my more inspired sermons had been on why chameleons change color.

"The title of this selection is 'Why We Are and Are Not Chameleons.' Our friend, the chameleon, can move his eyes in two different directions at the exact same time, sort of like Ivylee when she is looking at nude photos in the encyclopedia. We must not be chameleons though, because nobody here seems to experience a lot of change. In spite of the fact that some of us are flat, like Ivylee, and dark, like me, we still do not seem to be able to absorb any more light or heat to change our color. Chameleons will change color during the mating season or when they feel threatened or are trying to protect their territory. Since no one here, besides Momma, has ever legally mated, any possible color changes at those times could not be considered valid and certainly not binding. And although my sanity feels threatened every day, I cannot in good conscience say I would change color to protect this territory, even if I were a chameleon. If I couldn't run away, I would most likely always wear a white handkerchief around my neck for the purpose of surrendering and without the slightest moment's hesitation, which would surely not allow any time for changing color. But assuming by some strange quirk of fate I was a chameleon and did change color, my change would most likely be from lifeless brown to a dull gray, which seems to be my lot in life, regardless of my species. A chameleon that is feeling under the weather will stay pale, like Ivylee, because they just don't have the energy needed to flick their color wheel. Momma, on the other hand, reflects light wherever she goes, and if she were a chameleon, she would no doubt be a flashing neon sign."

While Momma gave me a standing round of applause, Ivylee stuck her tongue out at me so many times during my delivery, I could have easily believed the girl a lizard, sucking flies out of the air.

"Why, Sister," Momma declared, "That was delightful. Makes me want to run right out and find us a lizard. Why, we could name him 'Neon Leon' after your Uncle Leon. Wouldn't that just thrill him?"

Since Bunk was our daddy and was precious to Momma, she felt obliged to hold memorial services so that Ivylee and I would not forget Bunk. Momma also considered Bunk might need his leg again one day, and the best thing we could do for him was to hang on to his leg, which is what we did, hang on and remember. Religiously, we memorialized Bunk's leg like it was some sort of holy member of an ancient god lost in transit between worlds and waiting to be returned to its rightful deity. And that is what we did *every day*—wait in service for Bunk to come and collect his leg. "Why, I know he will be along any day now" became Momma's mantra, and we became the chorus, the props, and the backdrop and assumed our memorial service positions to be reminded that our daddy was Bunk, and Bunk was Precious.

Chapter 2

The Funny Farm

We live next door to a cemetery, not a claim everyone can make, not even in the South. As a neighborly gesture, Momma visits somebody's grave every day.

"My, my, that was exhausting." Momma plopped down on the sofa like she was a fifty-pound bag of potatoes.

"You don't need to be taxing your heart in this heat, Momma."

"I rearranged all the flowers in the graveyard. It looks so much prettier, and I'm sure Miss Ruby won't mind. She had so many pretty flowers, and she always was a generous sort. I took some of her flowers and placed them on the graves of some of those less fortunate souls, who don't have any flowers. Sad to think of those poor souls out there being ignored by their kin."

"One of these days, Momma, some of these folks' kinfolk are liable to catch you and be upset."

"Sister, a body's got to do what a body's got to do."

"Hogwash. Nobody has to do that."

Momma attends every funeral in town, which is not that unusual since she knows most of the people. After the graveside service when everybody has gone home, Momma "borrows" some of the flower sprays or baskets from the newly deceased's grave for the purpose of enhancing our service for Bunk's leg.

Momma pointed to the two plastic baskets of flowers setting on each side of our screen door. "You know, those flower sprays are beautiful, but these baskets are so much easier to carry. Why, I almost fell down with one of those funeral sprays the other day, right on top of poor Miss Peabody's grave. What would that dear lady think with me up there flailing around on top of her grave fighting with a funeral spray? I'll swannee, she'd probably just roll right over and look the other way, and I wouldn't blame her a'tol."

"Well, if you would just stick with the artificial flowers, you wouldn't have to worry with it. Better yet, if we would just bury the dang leg. . ."

"Sister, I've told you how I feel about that. Ain't no use going over it again. We cannot bury Bunk's leg with him still alive. It just ain't fittin'. Oh, but guess what? I got us two more artificial doves today. Isn't that wonderful?"

"We don't need anymore artificial doves, Momma. There's no more room."

"Well, Ivylee said I could hang some in her room."

"She would, the little twit."

"Now don't pout. I'll hang some in yours too."

"I don't want any artificial doves in my room, Momma. I don't want any artificial doves anywhere. I don't even want to see them on the funeral flowers in the graveyard. Why would anyone even a dead person need an artificial dove anyway? For that matter, why not an artificial hawk or an artificial crow or maybe an artificial cat?"

"An artificial cat! That's absurd, Sister. Now why would anybody put an artificial cat on a funeral wreath?"

"I would assume for the same reason they put an artificial dove."

"Sister, sometimes you just don't make no sense at all. Where do you get such strange ideas? Is it from that *National* magazine you're always reading? We gonna have to get you a more normal subscription. We are southerners, Sister, and southerners like artificial doves on their flower arrangements. It not only personalizes the arrangement, it adds a touch of sweetness to an otherwise difficult ordeal. You should know that."

With Momma's penchant for funerals, we have little white doves all over the place. Our living room looks like an artificial dove sanctuary.

"My, but isn't it lovely? I'll declare, it's like living in a birdhouse," Momma professes each time she ties white ribbon to another dove and hangs it from the ceiling.

With white, artificial doves in the house and white chickens in the chicken house, we are surrounded by lifeless or soon-to-be-dead birds. Along with the doves, the plastic baskets of funeral flowers, and our coffee table coffin, our living room would more likely be pictured in "House and Grave" rather than *Home and Garden*.

Besides the fact that our nearest neighbors are in the cemetery, our chicken farm is located along a tornado line. Through the years, we have watched many a tree upended and many a small building be blown away. As a result, unusual objects appear in our yard on occasion. With no other plausible explanation, we decided a tornado must drop this stuff.

"It's a sign for sure!"

"Momma, everything to you is a sign."

"It's the way God equips us to live in the world, dear."

"I thought He gave us 'The Ten Commandments' for that."

"Well, yes, but they don't quite cover everything. They're more like rules of the game, like when you play a board game. They write the rules on the box lid, but then you got to figure out where you gonna land and what you gonna do when you get there. They don't give you all that, and so you have to figure it out for yourself."

"Like what to do with Bunk's leg?"

"I got that one figured out, Sister. It's these other ones I'm working on now."

With her flowered bonnet tied to her head and singing ". . .I'm gonna take a trip on the good ole gospel ship. . ." Momma ponders and wanders the yard looking for clues. The woman has spent her entire life searching for signs.

When all this stuff started landing in the yard, Momma studied it like tea leaves in a teacup with the hope that it would give her some insight into the higher power's earthly plan.

The first piece to plant itself in our front yard was a gravestone. It landed halfway in the ground and upside-down. We couldn't read the name on the stone, but chiseled across it was: "HERE LIES AN ATHEIST, ALL DRESSED UP AND NO PLACE TO GO."

"How you reckon that gravestone got here?" Momma swept and dusted that gravestone like she was looking for fingerprints.

A gravestone landing in a person's front yard, especially a gravestone belonging to an atheist, is enough to give any Bible-belted Southerner pause for thought and caused Momma many a sleepless night.

"Let's just get rid of it, Momma. It's bad enough that

our nearest neighbors are dead. We shouldn't have to be reminded of that fact every time we walk out the front door."

"It might be a sign, and you cannot get rid of a sign, at least not until you know what it means. What puzzles me, Sister, is that I've never seen this gravestone. It surely must have come from next door, and I know every grave out there, so why haven't I ever seen it before?"

"Maybe the gravestone was buried too. Maybe somebody was ashamed of it."

"Guess that would make sense. I know it would shame me."

Although Momma accepted my explanation, she didn't seem to find a lot of comfort in it.

Not long after the gravestone landed, we found an old tree stump mantled across our front porch. The upside-down stump had roots shooting out in all directions like they were trying to grab onto something. Sprawled all across one side of our porch, that monstrous-looking thing gave the appearance of guarding our house like some sort of large, excavated, gone-mad Medusa. How it got there we don't know, and we're not at all convinced somebody didn't put it there.

"It's a sign for sure, a message from the Almighty. Wonder what it means?"

"Maybe it means you're supposed to get to the *root* of the problem."

"You might be right, Sister, but what is the problem?"

With her childlike innocence, Momma remained completely oblivious to her surroundings.

If the stump wasn't disturbing enough, smack dab in the middle of all those roots sat a doorknob encased in a board. It's one of those sights that stops you stone cold still, because the first thing that strikes you about it is that *it doesn't belong there.*

"This just ain't natural? A doorknob all tangled up in tree roots." Momma stood in front of that doorknob pondering it like a curious infant viewing its reflection for the first time.

Momma wasn't alone in her curiosity with this one. Initially, that doorknob gave all of us pause for thought. Every time your eyes encountered this unnatural sight, you found yourself drawn to it like a honeybee to clover, but a little frightened by it at the same time, like watching a horror movie—you *do, but don't* want to see it.

Every time Momma passed by that tree stump, she stopped and studied it. After a while, she began to knock on the board that encased the doorknob.

"Anybody there?" Momma asked after each knock with enough anxiety and anticipation in her voice to suggest the Grim Reaper waited on the other side.

The last piece to plant itself in our yard was a road sign. It landed all whop-sided at the edge of the yard.

"I never noticed that sign in the front yard before. Think I would have noticed a sign."

Momma brooded about that sign for hours, peering into it like it held some secret message she was supposed to share. At this point, there was no convincing her otherwise, especially since the sign read: "ONE WAY."

Momma fastened every facet of our lives onto that sign trying to figure out what was *one way*.

"Signs can't get any more real than being a sign, can they? But that don't help me understand it any better." Momma paced in the front yard as she repeated, "One Way."

On a regular basis, I asked Momma to let me have cousin, Harley, haul off all this stuff, and regularly Momma declined.

"We can't have it hauled off. It might be a message from God, and God wouldn't want us gettin' rid of his messages before we know what they mean. He might think they was something wrong with us."

Between these "signs," Bunk's amputated leg in the freezer, and the owner of that leg living out in the yard like a blessed bloodhound, it just got to be more than a rational person could comprehend, and as it was, Momma's allotment of rationality had never been vast. As a result, she became even more confused and irrational than before. She'd had a hard enough time when Bunk went berserk on her, and Momma just couldn't put all this other stuff into the mix with any sort of logical explanation. Every day the poor woman puzzled over what it all meant, but was no closer to an answer than the day before.

"I've looked up every one of these signs in the Bible, and I can't come up with any explanation I can understand."

"There is no explanation, Momma. It's just life, and sometimes life sends you mixed messages to trip you up."

"Well, then how am I supposed to know what is and what isn't? That don't help none, Sister. I may as well look for meaning in Ivylee's poetry if that's the case."

One afternoon while I was cleaning the windows in the living room, I looked outside to see Momma tying string from the gravestone to the doorknob to the One Way sign. For several minutes she stood in the center of this string triangle with her head tilted and looking up and her arms open as though to catch some angel plummeting to earth. After a while when nothing happened, she untied the string and came inside the house.

"Bless my soul, for the life of me, I can't seem to get a handle on why we have all this stuff."

"We have it because we haven't hauled it off." Without

a word, Momma dismissed my comment as though it were from a child on her way outside to play, and *play* is what we do here. We play at life, and while we play, we *wait*. Momma waits for Bunk to come reclaim his leg or for God to fetch her home.

Ivylee, whose brain is more likely damaged by laziness than a high fever, waits for an imaginary lover by the name of Mr. Robinson to come and whisk her away to her beautiful home in Miami.

Bunk waits, but no one knows for what. Although Bunk recovered from his gunshot wound, he still no longer knows who he is or even what he is some days. Like a blind puppy, our "Precious" Bunk wanders the yard, seemingly in search of something himself.

And me? I wait for relief, relief from running the family farm, a white, leghorn chicken farm whose residents are far flightier than the fowl themselves.

Bunk lost his leg; Ivylee recovered, but nothing in our lives was ever the same. Our respite from the reality of our lives is Momma's make believe, and I go along with it because it is easier than not going along with it. My job is to merely maintain what is fondly referred to as a "family," that beautiful, horrible collection of individuals who claim blood, if nothing else, as reason for being in one another's life.

To my knowledge, we have no skeletons in our closets. They are all out in the open, and roam about this farm like dazed inmates on the grounds of a state institution. So this is where we live: on a chicken farm in the rural South, next door to a cemetery, but far more *live* ghosts live on this farm and hold us hostage by blood obligation than dead ones that reside in the cemetery. Through the twists and turns of our fate, we find ourselves frozen in time, a time that Momma manages for us through make believe.

Chapter 3

Momma's Play

According to Momma, the sun shines down so bright on Joy that it surely must be dim someplace else. Our little community is simple, clean and well kept. We don't roll up our sidewalks at the end of each day; we decorate and prepare them for the next. As long as flowers bloom, they bloom in half, wooden barrels along the never-busy, two-lane streets of Joy, Georgia.

A red, white, and blue swirling sign in front of Joe's reminds folks that Joe still gives the best hair cut in town for the least amount of money. And Joe's is also where all the men folk congregate to swap tales, yet deny they gossip. Hair Haven promotes "sheik" to the female folk, who don't bother to deny much of anything, not that it would do any good even if they did.

My family is a frequent topic of conversation at both places, unfortunately. We not only fill the role of the town eccentric; we fill the role for the whole dang county.

If you want to know what's going on in Joy, you head on over to Hair Haven, and rumor has it that Sheriff Dorsey checks in regularly with Ruby to keep informed of the town's activities. Our Pick and Plume prepares flowers, fruit baskets, and gifts for almost any occasion that might arise. Mack's Barbecue Shack boasts the best barbecue in the region, and The Southern Lady feeds the hungry masses breakfast and lunch daily. Joy Hardware has everything an adventurous person might ever want in this part of the world, and a body can spend hours fingering its contents. At one end of town is a small, white, wood-frame church, First Baptist, and smack-dab at the opposite end of town sits the stately First Methodist. Both allow everybody in our closet community the opportunity to claim to be "first" at something.

The men folk tip their hats to the ladies, and we still say "sir" and "ma'am" when appropriate. With the exception of showing respect for our elders, everybody in Joy is on a first-name basis with everybody else, and everybody knows everybody else's business. If I need to know what's going on in my life, all I got to do is ask one of my neighbors. Of course that wouldn't be a hard one, because outside the oddity of my family, not that much goes on in my life. There are those who would say that given my family, my life is full, to which I would reply, "so is an outhouse, but that don't make it sweet."

We are 'all-my-lifers' in Joy. Ivylee and I were born here and have lived in Joy all our lives, not counting the two years I was away at school. Bunk, before he became Precious, was a simple man who provided a simple livelihood for his family. Our Momma was a housewife, a domestic engineer, who was quite adept at engineering our lives, and who, although sweet and kind, could be trying at times with her childlike innocence about most everything.

Momma borders on being something of a fanatic, although not necessarily religious, but more so when it comes to attending funerals. Momma attends them all, whether she knows the deceased or not. As a matter of fact, some of her best funerals have been for people she didn't even know. In a way, Momma has her own form of "frequent flyer," in that with her vast funeral experience, she could be considered a professional mourner, having logged in more hours sobbing and dabbing her eyes than probably any other person in this fair state.

Just last week, Momma and I attended a funeral for one of our former deacons, Brother Beebe, who had lived to the ripe, old age of ninety-three and for years had said that he was ready "to get on out of here." Of all the people that I have come to know in my life, Brother Beebe would have to be one of those who topped my list of favorites. With his up-front plain talk, he summed up situations with such simple and honest clarity that if what he said didn't tickle you, it would certainly give you pause to think. Basically, Brother Beebe said what the rest of us were either too polite or too cowardly to say.

Deacon or not, Brother Beebe practiced his own brand of Christianity and had never been one to "dress things up." Several years ago, Aunt Maisy, who no doubt could be best identified as the town gossip, stood up at Wednesday night prayer meeting and said how the church should pray for Brother Beebe. According to Momma, Aunt Maisy had been visiting a shut-in the day before and had seen Brother Beebe's red, pick-up truck parked in front of Pete's Tavern and Liquor Store.

"I'm telling you, brothers and sisters, it just ain't fittin' for a deacon of this church, or any other church for that matter, to be frequenting taverns and liquor stores." Momma allowed how Aunt Maisy went on to say that she thought Pastor Mike should speak to Brother Beebe. "Pastor, the way I see it, which would undoubtedly be how the Lord would see it, this sends a mighty poor message to our youth to have one of their church leaders visiting one of the devil's chambers."

According to Momma, in his usual soft-spoken and tactful way, Pastor Mike tried to convince Aunt Maisy otherwise. "Not a one of us besides Brother Beebe knows what he was doing at Pete's, Aunt Maisy, not to mention the fact that it is none of our business." But as is always the case, nothing that simple and straightforward was going to appease Aunt Maisy.

Momma said Aunt Maisy stood before Pastor Mike and the congregation with her self-righteousness all spread out and puffed up like a peafowl in heat. Aunt Maisy had found herself a mission, and she was in full march to right it. "Now Mike, what in the sam hill do you think he was doing there? I doubt if he was leading a prayer group or a Bible study class. He was doing the same thing everybody else parked in front of Pete's is doing—partaking of strong drink."

When tact could not alter the situation, as it never seemed to with Aunt Maisy, Pastor Mike shut down the discussion. "I don't presume to know what folks do when they are not in church, Aunt Maisy, and even if I did, I consider that a matter between them and God, and to be perfectly frank, I often wonder what some of them do when they are in church."

Momma said Aunt Maisy sat down in such a huff, "it was a wonder the folks sitting on the other end of her pew didn't get bounced slap up to the ceiling." Aunt Maisy surely had plenty to pray about that night.

Sheriff Dorsey, J.D., told me later that Brother Beebe had gotten wind of Aunt Maisy's tirade about his truck being parked in front of Pete's, and it didn't seem to set too well with him. "That night," according to J.D., "Brother Beebe drove his truck over to Aunt Maisy's some time after dark, when he was pretty sure she had gone to bed, and left his truck in her driveway all night and well into the morning." J.D. had been out making his rounds when he spotted Brother Beebe walking home, rolled his patrol car up beside him, and asked, "Your truck break down on you, sir?"

"Naw," J.D. said Brother Beebe answered as he rubbed his whiskered chin and then sprinkled the ground with brown spit from a chew of tobacco. "'Bout sun down, I went and parked my truck over in Maisy's driveway for the night. Seems to concern that woman where and what my truck is doing, so I was of the notion I'd give her something to explain to folks."

J.D. gave Brother Beebe a ride home. "You know she's gonna be mighty mad, Sir."

"Yep," J.D. said Brother Beebe replied. "I reckon she will. She might even call the law, J.D."

Brother Beebe always called it like he saw it, whether anyone happened to agree with his vision or not, and you couldn't help but respect his frankness. Had Brother Beebe not had a couple of generations on me, I think I would have married the man.

One Sunday morning, he was in front of us as we were leaving church, and I overheard Pastor Mike inquire as he shook Brother Beebe's hand, "Good morning, Brother Beebe, and how are you today?"

Without so much as a stammer, Brother Beebe replied, "Well, if I felt much worse, I couldn't be here, and if I felt much better, I wouldn't be here."

Pastor Mike smiled, but he had that kind of unsettled look a person gets upon realizing they have just stepped in something and messed up their shoe. Pastor Mike didn't ask Momma how she was doing that day.

Another time when Brother Beebe was entering the church ahead of us, he was greeted at the door by two of the ushers, both of whom happened to be members of the legal profession with offices at the county seat—with one being an attorney and the other a judge. Pastor Mike had been encouraging everyone who worked or helped out at the church to be a "joyful greeter" and to practice greeting folks in a warm and cheerful manner at every opportunity. So as soon as Judge Mabry spotted Brother Beebe coming inside, he said with all the warmth of a used car salesman, "Good morning, Brother Beebe. Welcome to church this fine Sunday morning."

Brother Beebe glanced first at Judge Mabry and then at the attorney. "If one usher is a judge and the other one's a lawyer, how's a body to be sure they in church?"

That same morning, Brother Beebe sat down on the pew in front of us. Gentleman that he was, he tipped his hat to Momma as he made his way to the opposite end of the pew, and Momma nodded in response. When Pastor Mike got to the place in the program where he directed us to turn and greet one another, Brother Beebe turned around with his hand extended to greet the person behind him, who happened to be Fletcher Fuques, the president of the local bank. Looking like he had just sucked the juice out of a lemon, Mr. Fuques responded, "I don't believe in this sort of thing, Beebe."

Brother Beebe stared at Mr. Fuques like he had just announced that he was a hermaphrodite. "My stars, man! What's wrong with you? Preacher ain't asking you to commit to marriage or to communism. He's asking you to shake hands in church and act like you know why you're here. And if you worryin' if I have cooties, I don't, and even if I did, I wouldn't give 'em to you anyway. Wouldn't set right with my conscience."

Mr. Fuques looked at Brother Beebe like he was a hobo who had happened through town and with a tilt of his banker's head, dismissed him as such.

Just about everybody in church heard Brother Beebe, and almost everybody was trying to stifle a giggle. Some folks pretended to be singing to keep from laughing out loud, in spite of the fact that what they were singing was not the same song the choir was singing.

Mr. Fuques was one of those folks considered to be a pillar of the community and had a say in just about everything that went on in the community. His family had done well in banking through the years and had passed down executive positions in the bank from one generation to the next. The Fuques were a tad uppity, a big tad, and some folks said they didn't talk to anybody who didn't have as much money as they did, which would eliminate most everybody in town. Brother Beebe knew this and appeared to enjoy jerking Mr. Fuques' chain at every opportunity. He was often heard saying, "Fletcher, if you ever had to work for a living, you'd starve to death."

When Mr. Fuques still refused to shake Brother Beebe's hand, Brother Beebe belted out, "'Blest be the tie that binds, Our hearts in Christian love. . ..'"

I thought I was going to explode, and Momma kept punching me in the side with her elbow to keep me from laughing out loud. "God bless, Brother Beebe." I leaned over and whispered in her ear. Momma tried to sing, but so many different songs were blaring together, it was hard to tell what to sing.

When Brother Beebe sat near us at church, I could trust that he would make the trip interesting if not downright funny. Brother Beebe was probably more entertaining in his eccentricities than anybody else in town. Of course, most people would probably say that my momma was more entertaining, but that would depend on a person's point of view.

Brother Beebe had always been kind to Momma. Years earlier, when he and his wife both came down with the flu at the same time, Momma prepared homemade soup every day and took it to them. Brother Beebe never forgot and never would, and no matter how bizarre Momma's action, Brother Beebe defended her. We were probably one of the few instances where he held his tongue. J.D. told me once that somebody in town had made some derogatory remark about Bunk in front of Brother Beebe when they were all at Joe's Barber Shop. J.D. said Brother Beebe picked up his hat, placed it on his head, walked to the door, and with his hand on the doorknob, turned and said, "Even as a zombie, he's still got more sense than most folks in this town."

Unlike Momma, I do not attend every funeral that happens along. Besides, Brother Beebe's, the last one I attended was for a former high school teacher of mine, Miss Pinky. Momma had left the house ahead of me, as she wanted to save us one of the pews with a better view, preferably the pew she considered to be hers, which she guarded like a blue jay after its babies. When I arrived, the choir was singing Miss Pinky's favorite hymn, "In the Garden." From the back of the church, I looked about for Momma, but did not see her on her regular pew or anywhere else. Concerned, I decided I had best look about the church grounds since as of last year, she had begun to have spells with her heart, and she also seemed to be a bit more confused of recent, although I am not sure an outsider could tell the difference. As I stood on the top step looking about the church grounds, my eyes were drawn in the direction of the graveyard, where a royal blue canopy

28

covered the open grave that awaited its new owner. Just as I was about to look elsewhere, I noticed movement underneath the canopy. At first, I assumed it was one of the gravediggers finishing up. On closer inspection, I spotted a head I recognized all too well surface out of the depth of that grave like a fishing bobble bobbing to the surface of a lake. Imagine my surprise to see the woman nearest and dearest to my heart hoist herself up by her elbows and pull herself out of Miss Pinky's soon-to-be-earthly bed. I was so mortified I lost the ability to move my body in any direction and could do nothing more than witness this abomination with my mouth open wide enough to catch any cardinals that might be flying by. The woman I had called "mother" all my life lifted her arms above her head, planted them on the artificial grass surrounding that gaping hole and ever-so-slowly pulled herself up and out of the depths of the grave. Like a winded, Olympic, long-distance runner, Momma collapsed onto the ground next to the mound of dirt that would soon blanket Miss Pinky's final resting place. After this temporary repose, Momma awkwardly pushed herself up from her knees, like a cripple with splints on both legs, and dusted herself off. Momma studied that hole in the ground like it was an automobile she was about to purchase. When the grave appeared to offer no answers to her ponderings, she straightened her hat, picked up her shawl and purse and meandered toward the front of the church, where I stood stiffer and certainly more shocked than Miss Pinky. When she reached the top step, Momma casually inquired, "Shall we go in now, Sister? It was sweet of you to wait for me."

Throughout the entire service, I was unable to focus on either poor Miss Pinky or the positive impact she had had on many of us. Instead, the image of my Momma climbing out of somebody else's grave took center stage in the theater of my mind, where it played over and over like some senseless fable with no plot or moral. My first thought was to take leave of the situation and head on over to the railroad tracks where I would either wait for a northbound train or simply lie down across the tracks in preparation for my own earthly bed. Having run away before, past experience reminded me otherwise, and I merely followed Momma inside like the simpleton I had come to be in recent years.

This was by far momma's greatest and most public preoccupation with death, and I had begun to wonder about the possibility of permanently putting away the woman who had given birth to me. My concern at the moment was whether it would be considered an inappropriate gift for Mother's Day and whether I should wear a white rose or a red one—while Momma was not completely dead, she certainly could not be considered alive. Maybe pink would be the more appropriate rose color for the day.

As we walked home that afternoon underneath a canopy of vibrant green where trees reached across the red, dirt road to touch their counterparts on the other side, I wanted to ask what and why, but wasn't at all sure I was prepared to hear the response. Some things in this world in their very action provide the answer, and any verbal response would only cause further confusion. I decided instead to look for maypops among the lush greenery alongside the road while Momma softly hummed "'Precious moments, how they linger. . ..'"

Chapter 4

Meet The Ninny

Later this same week, when I found myself chasing Precious, my mind returned to the railroad tracks and the opportunities they offered. I had finished feeding the chickens and was bolting the chicken house door behind me when I heard an automobile on the dirt road that wrapped itself around our farm. We do not see many cars on this road, so when one does pass, our curiosity is captured like a firefly in a Mason jar. Oddly enough, a hearse was driving past. Of greater concern was what was behind the hearse—Precious in hot pursuit. For some reason known only to God, Precious had decided to chase that hearse this morning. I took off running toward the road like a moon shiner with the law close behind. When I yelled for Ivylee to come and help me get Precious out of the road, the dingbat climbed on top of the well and started reciting some gibberish she had made up. The hearse driver, who was apparently lost, looked like he may have just stumbled across the home of Lizzie Borden. He swerved and weaved his long, white car on that narrow, dirt road like he was trying to prove sobriety to a State Patrol officer. He swerved and weaved not only to escape the nightmare in which he currently found himself, but also to keep from running over our Precious, who had somehow caught up with the car and was banging on the window. The poor man had to be paler than whomever he was hauling around in the back of his hearse and appeared scared out of his wits with eyes as wide and dark as open aluminum cans. Had the lost driver not been overwhelmed by the local natives on the warpath, he would have probably gotten out of his car and dropped to his knees in fervent, purposeful prayer.

When I was finally able to catch hold of Precious to lead him back to the house, I tried to apologize to the driver, but to my surprise, I found myself speechless. At first, I could neither apologize nor explain, although any explanation that could be considered acceptable would surely have been a challenge at best or a falsehood at worst.

In hindsight, I realize I learned something from this circumstance that I had not given previous thought to regarding my predicament. It is quite one thing to live in an environment where everyone for the most part accepts or even empathizes with your situation, but something else entirely when confronted by strangers with this same situation. Such was my dilemma this morning, along with the fact that the driver's nice, white, hearse was now covered in a fine red dust and lodged in a ditch in front of our farm. So I did what any self-respecting southerner would do. In a voice that could have dripped syrup, I tendered, "Sir, I am so sorry. You will have to forgive our Precious here. He became so excited when he saw your hearse, he no doubt thought it was for him, and as you can see, he is not quite ready to make so serious a commitment. Would you like to come up to the house for a glass of iced tea?"

The driver of the hearse looked at me like I might be speaking Egyptian, shook his head, backed out of the ditch and took off up the road like a jack rabbit with a coon hound behind it, all the while staying within the ditch lines of that narrow dirt road like the captain of a steamboat on a small river. While Precious waved goodbye, the big white hearse headed up the road, slinging red dirt in all directions.

After putting Precious in his place in more ways than one, I decided I needed that glass of ice tea myself. As if this was not enough excitement to begin our day, when I rounded the corner of the house to the front yard, I found Momma spread eagle on the ground in front of the upside-down gravestone. Before I could stop myself, I yelled at this woman with the heart condition, "Momma, what in tarnations are you doing?"

"I'm practicing," lifting her head to respond.

"Practicing what? How to be a loony bird? Don't nobody around here need to practice. We got that part down pat. Now get up from there this instant before somebody drives by, sees you, and calls the coroner, if they haven't already."

"I'm just looking for answers, Sister."

"Then go to the library. They got all kinds of answers there." This was simply more death in one day than a person should have to deal with.

As she pushed herself up on one elbow, Momma sighed, "Resting in peace ain't all that easy."

"And neither is living here, Momma. And you are just getting too weird for words. Now this has got to stop."

As I crossed the yard to help Momma to her feet, the dimwit joined us. "Ivylee, help me get her up."

While we were lifting her to her feet, Momma began to recite the "Twenty-Third Psalm." This is not all that unusual for Momma, as she recites Bible verses, or at least parts of them, throughout the day, but on this day, when she reached the part about "the shadow of death," she got confused and started singing, "Me and My Shadow." The "Twenty-Third Psalm" takes on a whole new image when the Lord takes off "strolling down the avenue" in "the valley of the shadow of death."

To Ivylee, these little mental excursions of Momma's seem nothing less than normal, and my greatest fear was becoming so accustomed to them that they might begin to take on the appearance of normal to me.

"Ivylee, you could have helped me with Precious," I fussed while Momma brushed herself off.

"I can't help you with something that ain't there, Sister."

Ivylee's standard response to anything she does not wish to deal with is to deny it even exists. For her, it doesn't exist, even if she runs smack dab into it every day, and when it came to Precious, he may as well have been a ghost in a halfway house to heaven on a different continent. "He's as there as you are, Ivylee, and some days, more so."

My cup was more than overflowing with the morning's events and my endurance level had reached its peak, so I decided it would be a good time to try to talk to Momma again about her morbid fascination with death. "Just because we live next door to a cemetery, Momma, doesn't mean we have to play dead." Bewildered, Momma looked at me like I had announced the end of time. "It's sorta like that question 'is the glass half-empty or half-full.'"

Before I barely had the words out of my mouth, Ivylee popped up with, "Half-empty or half-full of what?"

"It doesn't matter," I barked.

"Well, if it doesn't matter, then why did you ask?"

"Shut-up, Ivylee."

I was both delighted and surprised to hear Momma agree with me. "That's right," Momma concurred as she dusted the gravestone with a hanky she had in her apron pocket. "It don't matter, because whether it's half-empty or half-full, it's still half."

My temporary delight was as deflated as a hot-breath balloon flying through the air. Momma, having set me straight in this philosophical interlude I had introduced, crossed the yard to the porch and climbed the steps in the most nonchalant manner, dismissing my comment as though it were nothing more than a fair weather report.

"It does matter. It matters how you look at it."

"Well, I look at it this way." Momma removed the feather duster from one of the wooden pegs on the porch. "We live next door to a cemetery, and as far as I know, none of the graves are half-empty, and none of the coffins are half-full, except maybe for old man Potter's wife after she went on that trip. Hers might be half-empty."

The dimwit, who by now was perched on top of the gravestone like some cuckoo bird from a comic strip, was awakened from her usual stupor with this bit of information. "What trip?"

Despite my efforts to thwart the re-telling of this tale, Momma, who was now dusting our tree stump with the feather duster, explained, "You remember old man Potter, don't you? He owned the rubber plant and all them houses around it. They made tires and bicycle seats and handlebar grips, bouncy balls and all kinds of rubber stuff. And he lived in that big white house overlooking the Flint River. Mr. Potter was always doing some kind of community service and donated money to first one thing and then another. Folks was all-the-time trying to please him, and the town named a whole lotta places around here after him, like Potter's Park and The Rubber Room at the community center. Then all of a sudden, his wife up and died. Rumor got out that she killed herself with some rat poison, and they didn't bury her in the family plot. Buried her on the far side of the cemetery, right next to the river.

"It was that summer of all those awful rains. Rained for nearly three weeks straight without letting up. Water was everywhere, and what ground that wasn't under water was just saturated. Was sorta like walking on a waterbed in some places, although I've never walked on a waterbed, but I sat on one once. Was like sitting on gelatin. Why would anybody want to sleep on something that jiggled like gelatin? People surely get some strange notions. Water is not meant to sleep on; mattresses are meant to sleep on. You reckon that has anything to do with folks trying to be like Christ? They can't walk on water, so they make themselves a rubber bed and fill it full of water? Well, no matter, 'cause it's just not the same, is it?"

Momma looked up to see a puzzled Ivylee perched on top of the gravestone.

"Now where was I? Water, yes. Well, the ground was so wet with all that rain that some of them coffins on the far side of the cemetery floated up to the surface and into the river. Strange how that happened, and it was right peculiar seein' all those coffins floatin' down the Flint River like they was on a cruise to some celestial seaport. And 'Miz' Potter's coffin was one of them. Well, when old man Potter found out his wife was floatin' down the Flint River, he climbed on top of a barn and started shootin' at her. Filled her coffin plumb full of holes before they could stop him. When the law picked him up, he was muttering something, but nobody knew what it was. Poor Miz Potter's coffin sank to the bottom of the river, and for some reason, old man Potter wouldn't let nobody hoist it up. Probably still there.

"You know, we should take some flowers over and toss them in the river for Miz Potter. Some yellow and white chrysanthemums would be nice, and we could sing 'Shall We Gather at the River.' That would be fitting, wouldn't it?" Momma looked toward me for approval, and when I did not respond, she added, "Anyways, her coffin might be half-empty."

Throughout Momma's recitation, Ivylee had been painting her toenails with a bottle of fingernail polish she had placed in her pocket that morning. From atop the gravestone, Ivylee stretched her leg out and pointed her toes to admire her handiwork, and then with all the simplicity of a simple-minded moron sighed, "Sounds like a beautiful love story to me."

That's what she said: "A beautiful love story." I usually try to avoid any conversation with Ivylee whatsoever, as I find it about as insightful and rewarding as talking to a termite, but I was unable to restrain myself. "Ivylee, the woman killed herself with rat poison, and her husband filled her coffin full of bullet holes. What's beautiful about that?"

"Maybe he didn't want her to leave him, to go floatin' away all by herself down the Flint River."

I chose not to respond to this because doing so would only inspire greater stupidity.

"'From dust-to-dust,'" Momma declared as she continued to dust the tree stump like it was a piece of fine furniture. "Wonder what it was Miz Potter did to make old man Potter shoot her, even after she was already dead?"

"What makes you think she did anything? The woman didn't take rat poison for no reason." Seizing the opportunity, I planted myself in front of Momma. "They're dead, Momma, but we're not. Death will come without our waiting for it. The coffin is only half-full."

"Of course it's only half-full," the ninny echoed. "All we got is his leg."

The moment was not only gone, it had been emasculated by the nitwit.

"Oh, that reminds me, girls. I got some new ideas for our memorial service this morning."

"The best idea for our memorial service is not to have it."

Momma patted me on the cheek like I had tried to play a trick on her. "Why, whatever would we do if we didn't have the service, Sister?"

"Oh, I don't know. Maybe something mundane like living I suppose." While Momma re-hung the feather duster on the wooden peg, I made yet one more vain attempt. To help her focus, I turned Momma to face me and placed my hands on her shoulders. "Let's bury the leg."

"Ain't no need," the ninny offered. "She'd just dig it up."

Living with Ivylee is sort of like living with an obnoxious parrot. At the most inopportune times, the odious bird may say anything.

"When Bunk says we can bury the leg, Sister, we'll bury it."

"Bunk's not here, Momma. He's gone and may never come back, and memorializing his leg is not going to bring him back. Bunk is Precious now, and that's all he is."

"I know, dear," Momma responded with a soft, hopeless look of pain before regaining her composure. "Why did you say you were chasing Precious this morning?"

Defeated, I removed the broom leaning against the wall and began to sweep the porch. "He was running after a hearse when it went by, shouting something nobody could understand. Driver ran smack dab into the ditch trying to keep from hitting him."

"Wonder what a hearse was doing here," Momma pondered.

"He was lost and apparently took a wrong turn in town. But something about it sure didn't set right with Precious."

"Oh, the poor baby," Momma sympathized. "Must have confused him awful bad. He may have thought it was coming for him."

After turning her toes into what looked like plastic holly berries, Ivylee relocated and was now sitting on the steps of the front porch. "Probably nothing there. Never is."

"Just because you don't want something to be there, Ivylee, don't mean it's not. He's there, and he'll always be there until Momma agrees to have him hauled off to the funny farm." As I swept the dust in Ivylee's direction, she removed a scarf from her neck and tied it around her head, most likely to keep her small brain from falling out.

"Maybe Precious was speaking in tongues. Maybe that's why you couldn't understand him." Momma studied the tree stump for a moment, and then knocked on the board surrounding the doorknob. "Anybody there?" When no one answered, she tried turning the knob.

"Momma, it's a doorknob, not a door. There's nobody there. It's not the Oracle of Delphi. You're not going to get an answer."

"The Oracle of Delphi," Ivylee repeated. "Are you reading comic books again? I thought you outgrew that."

The scarf did not appear to be doing its job, but with something so small, not much can be expected.

"And I thought you said this was the funny farm?" the nitwit asked.

"No, this is not the funny farm. It's just that everybody on it has turned funny."

"Excuse me, you're the one reading comic books again."

Trying to talk to either of them carried with it more frustration than one person can endure over any length of time. So I concentrated my efforts on simply sweeping the porch, in Ivylee's direction.

From an old icebox that sat to the right of the screen door, Momma removed a basket containing a pastel-colored egg carton and a pair of scissors. Like paper dolls, Momma cut the egg pockets from the carton one at a time while she hummed her favorite hymn, "Standing on the Promises of Love." Also inside the basket were flower arrangement sticks she had removed from funeral flowers in the cemetery. One at a time, Momma pushed each egg pocket onto one of the funeral flower sticks until each of the twelve pockets had been poked onto the end of a stick. With her basket of egg carton creations on her arm, Momma descended the steps to the shrubs that lined our front porch, where she pushed one egg carton pocket creation after another into the branches of the boxwood shrubs. Pleased with herself, Momma stood back to admire her work. Our Styrofoam flowers this week were a sea foam green.

Recently, I had begun to worry that our situation was nearing a state of desperation, since Momma seemed to regress further each day into a world of her own making. Unwilling to accept total defeat, with one more effort, I ventured, "Let's sell the farm, Momma, and move to Atlanta."

"Sell the farm. How would we ever survive without the farm? It's the only thing we know how to do."

Ivylee removed one of Momma's egg carton flower creations from a boxwood bush and placed it behind her ear. "Not me. I don't know how to farm. I'm a poet."

"You're a twit, Ivylee, not a poet."

"You must like that shade of green. You always got it on."

"Girls, let's not bicker," Momma interrupted. "Let's make it a pretty day."

"The day I'm jealous of you, Ivylee, is the day you get off this farm, which is about as likely as your sprouting wings."

As Momma placed the flower basket back inside the icebox, her attention was once again turned to the tree stump. "You think this thing will ever root?"

"It's upside-down, Momma. And it's a tree stump. Exactly what do you think it's going to root to? The roof?" I stopped sweeping long enough to look at Momma in the hope I had misheard what she had said.

"Maybe it could root to heaven," the parrot proffered.

"Oh, what a lovely thought. Sister, you should try to think lovely thoughts like Ivylee."

"I'd rather think nothing at all," I muttered.

From the icebox, Momma removed an old, ornate, electric clock, whose face was centered in the belly of a rooster, and placed it among the roots of the tree stump.

With the ability to add a bit of idiocy to any moment, Ivylee stood at the top of the steps. "How do you like this one, Momma? 'Between heaven and hell, there is God. Between God and me, there is reality.'"

"That was just darling, dear." Momma smiled and applauded. "You know, you should write a poem about our root, Ivylee."

At one and the same time, Ivylee smiled, and in a condescending manner, assured Momma that she would consider the suggestion.

Momma focused her attention on polishing the rooster clock. Like Ivylee, the rooster clock did not work and had not worked in years. Actually, I don't recall the clock ever working, but each day, Momma would place her ear next to the rooster's belly and with all the surprise of a kid with a jack-in-the-box that refused to jump, proclaim, "What? No time again today? Well, we can wait. What time do we want it to be, girls?"

Each day, I would ask what difference it made because it didn't work and would suggest we get rid of it, and each day, Momma, with all the sincerity of a cow chewing its cud, would respond, "We wouldn't know what time it was."

"If it doesn't work, we don't know what time it is anyway."

The place in this conversation where I generally surrendered was when Momma would respond, "My point exactly."

More times than I care to consider, the woman has explained her reason for not being able to get rid of the clock, and at none of those times has her reasoning appeared anywhere close to sensible. "I've had it all my life. When I was little, it would 'who-who' on the hour. I used to lay in bed and count the who-whos and wonder who myself."

As though she had been startled awake, Ivylee jumped up, ran across the yard, climbed on top of the gravestone and echoed, "Who-who, who-who, who-who. The rooster sits in a tree, sits there calling me, and sings 'who-who, who-who, who-who,' and I wonder who, who can it be."

Most people would conclude that given our family, this would not or should not be a surprise, and understandably so. But until you have seen one of your relatives, no matter how dimwitted, standing on top of a gravestone 'who-ing,' well, it simply defies logic, no matter how jaded you may have become by trying to sustain your pitiful existence under such hopeless circumstances. Momma applauded, and Ivylee bowed.

"Momma, *owls* 'who;' roosters crow."

Momma placed her finger ·aside her mouth to ponder this like it was a reminder of an important task she had overlooked. "I know. That always did seem odd to me. I asked my daddy about it once, and he said he reckoned that somewhere in the world an owl was crowing and to always be on the lookout. Anyway, you can't get rid of something just because it don't work, Sister. You never know when it might work again. And besides, I've always known what time it was. As long as we're alive, it's our time."

"You can't be sure of that," I said.

"That it's our time?"

"No, that we're alive."

As she stepped down from the gravestone, Ivylee offered proof, not necessarily of life, but of dementia. "When I wake up in the morning, and I look into the mirror and see somebody's there, I assume it's me, so I know I'm alive."

Ivylee's proof is proof-positive that there is some logic behind why some animals eat their young. Although all of my existential concerns could certainly <u>now</u> be laid to rest, before I could respond, Momma chanted, ". . .'cause the Bible tells me so."

"Da-dum," Ivylee shouted as she swung open her arms and plopped her body down onto the steps of the porch like a busted fifty-pound bag of cornmeal. "You're not going to give us anymore of that stupid talk again today, are you? I wish Momma and Bunk had never let you go off to that ole school. All you talk about is stuff that don't even deserve the time it takes to run through our heads."

I swept more dust and dirt in Ivylee's direction. "In your case, that's not very long since there's nothing in

43

yours to slow it down."

Ivylee stood, dusted herself off, and with her hands on her hips, looked like she might, at any moment, turn into a whirligig. And I, with something close to malice in my heart, wished she would and with a big gust of wind would be blown away, to Oz maybe, where they are surely short a witch.

With as much logic as Ivylee is capable, she defended her pitiful self. "I am not feeble-minded. If I were, Mr. Robinson could not have loved me so much. That man would have died for me."

"Appears he did, Ivylee. Do you see a Mr. Robinson around here?"

"My Mr. Robinson is not dead. How dare you suggest such a vulgar thing. He'll be along any day now to get me and take me back to our beautiful home in Miami."

"Ivylee, Mr. Robinson doesn't exist."

Momma, who has heard this argument more times than mites on a chicken, dismissed it with greater ease than unencumbered breathing. With her attention focused on the oversized root arrangement on our front porch, she removed the flowered hanky from her pocket and proceeded to spit-shine the doorknob. After the hands on the clock had been set to whatever the appointed time, Momma stepped back to admire her shiny doorknob in her just-dusted tree stump with her newly-polished rooster clock that used to 'who' when she was a child. And such was Momma's version of art imitating life.

"You know what, girls? We've never had a sunrise service. Wouldn't that be fun? Bunk's birthday is coming up, and I know he would just love a sunrise service."

"Bunk is not here. Remember? We got Precious now."

"But he would be here if he could be, Sister."

I wanted to add "yes, but I wouldn't be if I could," but

decided the comment would do nothing more than open the door to further discussion disasters. Frustrated, I went inside the house. Unfortunately, the two dark delusional clouds, who decorate this futile fairy tale, followed me inside.

Chapter 5

Welcome To The House
On 'Who-Who' Hill

L ife on a farm begins at dawn. The day begins with feeding and caring for the chickens and ends with feeding and caring for the chickens. Most chicken farmers raise chickens from baby chicks to full-grown chickens in nine weeks. At the end of the nine weeks, the chickens are sold and then slaughtered. Although I try not to think about that part of the process, it has never ceased to disturb me, no matter how long we have maintained our meager existence by this means.

The two weeks between selling a batch of chickens and before receiving a new batch of baby chicks is spent preparing the chicken house. The dirty wood shavings and droppings have to be removed, and new shavings spread on the hard, dirt ground. Corrugated box tops have to be folded to hold chicken feed for baby chicks; water jars have to be washed and filled with fresh water; brooders have to be lowered and lit for each community of chicks that lives underneath and around an individual brooder. Although little used initially, water troughs have to be lowered and washed.

By the time baby chicks arrive from the hatchery, the shavings in the chicken house are new and clean, and the smell of freshly shaven wood fills the air. The crisp, pungent smell of the wood shavings is so strong that it can easily transport memory to another time, another place—a sawmill where two young girls ran and jumped and slid on the mounds of sawdust until their bare legs turned rose red and burned from irritation, all while their daddy negotiated price and number of loads.

Running a farm is a continuously repetitive process. Most days the work is the same as the day before. Necessity dictates life, and even with a lack of intention, patterns and habits develop with little or no deviation. In general, I try to keep myself busy, to be unaware of either my life or my surroundings. Toil can dull the sharp edges of anxiety and diminish thoughts. Work will eat the hours until the day is devoured, and exhaustion will smother any longing onto the pillow that awaits. Day coasts into dusk, and dusk into darkness, where night gives way to sleep and to absence of thought, until dawn breaks, and escape is interrupted. Years pass with such similarity that one is no more distinguishable from the last nor will it be from the next.

"Busy hands are happy hands," according to Momma. My wish is that my "happy hands" would channel to the rest of me. Instead, I must merely be the conduit for happiness channeling to the chickens, as they appear more at peace in their short nine weeks than I in my many years so far.

When finished with my morning chores in the chicken house, I turn my attention to the other house, whose occupants are far less easy to maintain. Just as in the chicken house, in the same, almost mechanical fashion, I perform my chores, a lot of which occur in our living room, the room where the three of us spend most of our time together. I view this room with the small coffin that serves as a coffee table, the baskets of wilting funeral flowers, the dilapidated stove that serves as a stage, and the hundreds of artificial doves hanging from the ceiling, as if it were a bee sting on my subconscious that is covered with mud, but the mud has yet to draw the pain or the stinger out. As our living room could probably pass as Dr. Frankenstein's family room of domesticated warmth and comfort, I try not to look at it and certainly not to think about it. It may be the room where we live, but in my mind, it is a room in some motel in a far off place operated by eccentric owners, who most likely suffer from some kind of mental malfunction.

From the front porch, Momma and Ivylee followed me inside the house. Momma continued to chatter while I removed the iron and ironing board from the closet. "Couldn't you just do this one sunrise service for Bunk, Sister? It would mean so much to him."

"Bunk is not here, and sunrise is too early to be singing hymns."

"It's never too early to sing hymns."

"Over a dead leg it is."

To soothe herself, Momma sat on the sofa, leaned forward and stroked the coffin. "And Bunk *is* here. He's just not like he used to be. Why, I'll bet he'll be his old self again any day now. Just you wait and see."

Ivylee plopped into the overstuffed chair like a clumsy duck landing on water. Again, she took on her parrot role as she mimicked whatever it was she thought Momma wanted her to say. "Well, I think a sunrise service would be lovely. I could recite one of my morning poems, and we could have some apple fritters afterwards. Hand me my magazine while you're there please, Momma."

Momma stood and lifted one of the sofa cushions to remove Ivylee's monthly installment of pure, unadulterated nonsense. "You are such a comfort to me in my hour of need, Honey."

Momma lifted the lid on the coffin and removed her Bible. "Your hour of need spans the better part of a decade, Momma. Ever since do-do bird here ran that high fever and fried her brain, and you made me come home to run this God-forsaken farm."

"I don't think this farm is God-forsaken," Momma chirped like a little chickadee who might have been jolted out of its nest. "Do you think our farm is God-forsaken, Ivylee?"

Absorbed in her magazine, one so worthless that even a bird would refuse to poop on it, Ivylee parroted, "Of course not, Momma. I'm sure God's out there somewhere. What would all those dead people be doing out there if he weren't? Oh, I only have two more stories, and then I'll have to wait for my next installment."

"Momma, you are asking someone whose greatest accomplishment is reading a story about aliens who impregnate toads."

"It was a frog that impregnated a girl who was swimming in a lake somewhere up north. Wouldn't you know something like that would happen up north? Yankees are just so peculiar. Bless their hearts, I guess they just can't help it. Anyway, they said the baby was half-human and half-frog."

"Ivylee, don't you know that stuff's not true?"

"Well, they wouldn't print it if it wasn't true, Sister.

Didn't you learn anything while you were in school?"

Due to the fact that flinging a hot iron at a demented relation would not be considered the better part of valor, I decided to shut down for the time being. Even so, I ironed clothes with such intensity that I could have been pressing the queen's costume for the fourth of July parade, that is, if the South could lay claim to a queen, other than the one in our living room who perceived herself as such.

Later that same morning, I was in the kitchen preparing some Mason jars to can our summer peaches. On top of the stove, water bubbled and boiled in a shallow pan whose bottom I had cushioned with newspaper. Just as I placed the last jar to be sterilized upside down in the pan of boiling water, I heard a knock at the door. A few minutes later, when another knock sounded, I stepped into the hall to see if either of them was going to answer the door. Momma sat wide-eyed in the center of the sofa looking as though she had surprised herself by laying an ostrich egg. Ivylee, who was so absorbed in her magazine that I thought she might have been reading naughty tales about herself, did not appear to be aware of a knock or a door or even of the world for that matter.

"Are either of you going to get that? Or are you just going to think about it?"

When I interrupted Ivylee's outrageous tabloid bliss, she looked like a child who had stumbled across some unusual object in the yard. "I wonder who it could be."

With her Bible over her head, Momma whispered, "Might be him."

"Who?" I asked as I stomped across the living room.

From beneath her Bible, Momma pointed upward.

"Yes, and it might be 'The Wizard of Oz' come to give us a brain. Get hold of yourself, Momma" When I opened the screen door, there was no one there, but lying on the front porch near the door, I noticed a rock with paper wrapped and tied with string. "What's this? Wonder who it's from." As I untied the string, Momma and Ivylee joined me at the door.

Our resident specialist on girls impregnated by frogs shrieked, "Oh, I'll bet it's from my Mr. Robinson." Even Momma looked taken aback by that one.

On the wrinkled paper, scratched in rough print was, "It's me. I want to come back."

Unbeknown to Momma and Ivylee, I had been romantically involved with the chicken doctor, who inspected our chickens. To my regret, the man was married. Although I knew this involvement to be morally wrong, I could not bring myself to believe the hell I would inherit would be any worse than the one in which I currently resided, so I told myself differently and looked anywhere but at the silver band on his finger. With a heart filled to the brim with longing for both love and the chance to leave, I wanted him to be married to me. At our last rendezvous, when the subject of his matrimonial state came up yet again, the conversation did not go as I would have liked, and he left on an unsettling note. As I read those words on the wrinkled paper, along with Ivylee, I, too, concluded, "It's probably for me."

"And who would send you a note?" Ivylee asked with such astonishment in her voice as if to render the possibility impossible.

Before I could respond, Momma, with her arms opened to receive air or a bolt of lightning, burst into song. "'Rock of Ages, cleft for me. Let me hide myself in Thee. . .'" Momma stopped singing as abruptly as she had started and studied the rock like it was a magic box. "Except I don't think I can hide in there. Kinda small." With the rock clutched against her bosom, she blared, "'. . .Save from guilt and make me pure.'"

"Get hold of yourself, Momma."

"What do you think we should do with it?" Momma asked as though we had found some alien child hiding on our premises.

"Well, why don't we blanche it and have it for supper? What'd you mean what should we do with it? We have to figure out who it's from."

"Maybe it's from God."

"I think your mind has finally gone all way round the bend, Momma. God does not go around leaving messages tied to rocks on people's porches."

"Maybe he had Moses do it."

Ivylee giggled like she had heard a knee-slapper. "She's got you there. And besides, you don't know what God does."

"You're right there, because if I did, maybe I could better understand why I am here."

"Maybe it's from Bunk."

"It'd sooner be from Moses," I replied.

"Well, it could be from Bunk. But I think it's from God. He's been looking for me."

"Why? Did you check out a hymnal and forget to return it? If God hasn't found you in all this time, Momma, it's not likely that He's been looking for you."

With all the insight of an earthworm, Ivylee remarked, "Maybe they been playing hide and seek."

So as not to slap her and to change the subject, I announced, "The chicken doctor is scheduled to inspect the chickens today, and I need to finish my chores."

"He just inspected the chickens," Ivylee declared. "What's he trying to do? Get them ready to join the Peace Corps?"

"I don't think chickens can join the Peace Corps, can

they?" Momma asked.

Lost once again in the rhinestones of her magazine, I decided it best to let this one slide. I doubted if Ivylee had any idea what the Peace Corps was, and it was not a subject I cared to explain to her. To her, the Peace Corps could be a fruit farm where pieces of apples are cored for cider.

While I folded the note and placed it inside my shirt pocket, Momma placed the rock on top of the coffin and stood back to study it from different positions around the room. When no insight as to the who, what, or why of the rock came to her, she shook her head and ambled across the room to the sideboard. From a cupboard, Momma removed her sewing basket. With the basket in her lap, she removed a sheet of black construction paper, which she cut into strips, folded the strips into circles and interlocked the circles with glue onto a strand of already completed black garland. For reasons probably best not thought about, Momma and Ivylee were forever making paper creations.

One night when I went to the chicken house to raise the curtains, I found bright-colored origami angels hanging in each window of the chicken house. With artificial doves in the living room and paper angels in the chicken house, I also came to believe that it must be a "sign," a sign our family must surely live somewhere in the ozone layer where paper creations were sent to safety before environmental terrorists could capture and return them to pulp. Were I more than moderately spiritual, I might have dropped to my knees right there in front of the feed bin that night and asked God for meaning.

While I poked a piece of cotton into a small tear in the screen of the screen door to keep the flies from entering the house and while Momma continued to loop black strips of paper into circles, Ivylee snapped to attention as though jolted by an electrical shock. Studying her rag of a magazine, she said, "You know, I think I'll order me one of these breast developers. They're guaranteed to work, and just look at this girl." She leaned forward to show Momma the before-picture of a homely-looking, flat-chested girl, who after using the so-called "breast developer," not only became so busty that her bosom was pushing its way out of her scanty clothes, but who was also transformed into a beautiful, sexy woman fit to perform in any Las Vegas night club. "This is before, and see. She didn't even have as much as I do, and would you look at her now! Just amazing what science can do for you these days. And to think, I didn't even like science when I was in school. Of course, I used to think it was all just dissecting frogs and pigs. Can you imagine doing a thing like that for the rest of your life?"

I may have let that last one slide, but no way was I going to let this one pass. "If it's any comfort to you, Ivylee, I can't imagine you doing any kind of work for the rest of your life."

Momma, who tries to take advantage of any opportunity to uplift her daughters, felt called to stroke Ivylee's self-image. "You'll never have to do a thing like that, Honey, because you got a real talent, and people with a real talent don't have to do low-life stuff like that. And she *is* trying to get a job, Sister."

I, on the other hand, seek no opportunity to assist Ivylee in feeling regarded any higher than a toadstool. "The job Ivylee is trying to get, Momma, doesn't exist. You can't get a job that doesn't exist."

"Why, thank you, Momma," Ivylee sweet talked to Momma before turning her attention to me. "And it's not my fault if there aren't any jobs for poets advertised in the paper." Ivylee punctuated her sentence by sticking her tongue out at me.

Almost hourly it sometimes seemed, Momma would ask me to look outside and see what Precious was doing, and almost hourly, I would tell her to let Ivylee see what he was doing because, according to her, Precious was Ivylee's "little gift" from Mr. Robinson. As Mr. Robinson does not exist, it would follow that he had not given Precious to Ivylee, but because this was a source of much torture to Ivylee, I reminded her often.

When Ivylee was sick and delirious, she convinced herself that there was a Mr. Robinson in her life. Because it seemed to provide her some comfort, Momma went along with this delusion, but for reasons only Momma could wrap her mind around, she decided to tell Ivylee that Precious was a gift for her from Mr. Robinson. Ivylee, on the other hand, had more use for a magpie than she did for Precious. Her disdain for Precious was considerable, as he did not fit into her fantasy or her life as far as she was concerned. Precious was about as appealing to Ivylee as a case of chicken pox. "Precious is not mine! The only thing that's mine is Mr. Robinson. And just as soon as he returns. . ."

Since pleasure is a relative emotion, I took every opportunity to interrupt this delusion. "And tell me, Ivylee, when is that going to be?"

"He'll be along any day now."

"It's been 'any day now' for nine years. Don't you think you need a new game?"

"I told you, Mr. Robinson is working on a big real estate deal over in New Orleans, and just as soon as he closes the deal, he's gonna come get me and take me back to our beautiful home in Miami."

"He could have closed on the Louisiana Purchase by now." Having had my fill of family time, both in quantity and quality, I removed my straw hat from the coat rack to go gather corn from the garden. Momma wanted to make chow-chow tomorrow, and in the garden, I didn't have to listen to or converse with the corn.

Chapter 6

Secret's Out

Just as many times a day as Momma tells me to look and see what Precious is doing, she goes to the screen door to see for herself. "Precious, what have you got there? You know, I think he's got a snake. Put that thing down, Hon. We don't practice snake handling in this family. That's not part of who we are. Now put it down."

While I folded the remaining clothes in the laundry basket, Ivylee pulled a large, white, paper contraption she had been weaving and working on for months from underneath the sofa. "You know, Momma, I been thinking we should have a Standard Home Party. We could invite all the neighbors and have some pound cake and some ice-cream punch. We could even get some new things for the house like that stuff you put in the toilet to make the water turn purple."

"Why in God's name would anyone want the water in their toilet bowl to be purple? Purple is the color of grape

57

juice. Why would anyone want to tinkle on what looked like their juice?"

"You are so insensitive to your surroundings, Sister."

At this point, I stopped and stared at her like she might be eating hornets. "This is a chicken farm. As such, exactly how sensitive do you think I should be? Should we put lace doilies on the chicken brooders? Or maybe we could hang a chandelier over the feed bin? Maybe you could crochet some little booties for the little chicken's feet."

"I'm not talking about the chicken house. You don't live in the chicken house."

"Are you sure? I'm out there seven or eight hours a day."

"It's the artist in her, Sister," Momma whispered. "Artists like to be surrounded by color."

"In the toilet bowl?"

Undaunted by any sense of reality, Ivylee continued her own little mental excursion. "Maybe we could even get some of that new perfume they have out. What is that stuff called? 'Moonflower,' that's what it's called. Oh, I'll bet it smells just heavenly. Maybe like moonbeams."

For no other reason other than to break the monotony of the moment, I joined in the conversation. "Moonbeams don't smell."

"You don't know that. You've never been to the moon."

"Ivylee, while I don't doubt your credentials when it comes to space, don't you ever wonder about a company that makes toilet bowl cleaner and perfume under the same roof? What if some jerk got drunk on the job one night and put toilet bowl cleaner in the perfume bottles? Your ears would be sitting up there on the side of your head just waiting to be flushed, but in your case that would probably be an improvement."

With doe-eyed innocence, Momma looked up from the open Bible in her lap. "If he's drinking on the job, I think they should fire him. Somebody could get hurt." Momma reached over and stroked the coffin. "Oh, my poor Bunk. I miss him so. Maybe we should. . ."

"Not this early in the day, Momma."

"Well, you shouldn't have brought it up," Ivylee reminded. "You said the man was drinking on the job and had an accident. And Bunk had an accident."

Momma sighed as she leaned forward and stroked the coffin again.

"I don't know if the man was drinking on the job or not. I was just using him as a hypothetical situation."

"A what situation?" the ninny asked as she continued to work on the white paper contraption in her lap. "You don't even know what that word means."

"You shouldn't be spreading rumors about people, Sister, if you don't know if they are true or not."

"Momma, I don't know the man. I don't know where the company is. And I don't know why we're having this conversation."

"Then why are you spreading rumors about somebody you don't even know? Isn't that just like her, Momma?"

It occurred to me to choke Ivylee at that moment, but I restrained myself and settled for ordering her to stay out of it. "Shut-up, Ivylee."

"Ivylee's right, Sister. You ought not to gossip about people you don't know. You could cause that man to lose his job."

"I wasn't gossiping about him. He doesn't even exist. I was just using him as an example."

"An example of what?" Momma picked up the rock again, studied it, placed it inside her Bible and tried to close the book like she might be pressing a flower memento from some fond occasion. "Is this some more of that psycho stuff you were reading to me? Like when that man was teaching his dog to slobber when he rang a bell?"

"Why on earth would anyone want to teach their dog to slobber?"

"A person with a pet can make a lot of money, Ivylee."

Somewhere in this conversation, I began to believe that I was not only their sustainer, but in some convoluted, warped way, I had become their source of entertainment. "I'm not going to try to explain this to you, Ivylee, because I don't think I can make it that simple."

"Will you stop treating me like I'm simple-minded? Just because Momma let you go off to that ole school, you think you are the only one that knows things. It's a good thing she made you come home when Bunk went berserk or you'd be even more uppity than you are now. And I'll have you know that I know things too. I just don't flaunt mine like you do. I don't have to. I've had a man. I don't have to pretend like it don't matter."

Whenever the subject of sex came up, Momma would usually find some excuse to exit. "I'd better go check on Precious. He's not a snake handler, and I sure don't want him messing with no snake." She removed the rock from her Bible and placed it in her apron pocket. "Maybe I'll ask Precious if he knows who sent us this rock."

"It don't matter to you, Ivylee. You'd have sex with a corpse and call it a gangbang. You even got it on with goofy, ole Bobby Ray Rittock when he was all broken out with poison ivy."

"I told you I didn't know he had poison ivy. I thought he was just nervous. And that only happened because I miss my Mr. Robinson so."

"Mr. Robinson is nothing more than a product of your weak mind."

Like an annoying jingle that plays over and over in your head, Ivylee chanted, "Only to you because you can't have him. I remember all too well how you used to flirt with my Mr. Robinson, even after our beautiful wedding."

"Ivylee, you didn't have a beautiful wedding. You don't have a beautiful home in Miami. You ain't never been to Miami, and you ain't no more married to Mr. Robinson than you are an awarding-winning actress in a soap opera, except for the one that plays in your feeble mind."

With her innate ability to reduce deductive reasoning to nonsense, Ivylee twittered, "Well, I'm more married to him than you are, and I can prove it."

"How? By making up more stories about a wonderful sex life with a man that grew out of a delusion years ago? There was no Mr. Robinson, Ivylee. You were delirious, and Momma just went along with it."

"I don't make up stories about something as serious as sex."

Sex was like an elusive firefly to Ivylee—every time she thought she'd captured one that was lit up, it stopped blinking on her. "You don't have to prove you're a tramp, Ivylee. From the time you could toddle, we have known that. You used to take your panties off and hang upside-down on the barnyard gate waiting for the school bus to come by. Embarrassed me no end."

"I told you I never did that."

"Guess I saw for myself. Never seen anybody who liked to show off as much with so little to show."

"I can't help it if my muffins are bigger than yours."

"They are not bigger. And they are not muffins. They are breasts!"

"Well, my Mr. Robinson refers to them as his little muffins. He likes to caress them in the morning when we first wake up in our king-size bed in our beautiful home in Miami."

As I pondered what ring of purgatory I had reached at this point in my life or death, I muttered, "Pancakes'd be more like it."

Like a mosquito on a mission, Ivylee laid her paper contraption aside, pranced over to where I was ironing, and pushed her chest forward like she was being sucked boobs-first into a wind tunnel. "Well, I'll compare my pancakes to yours anytime."

"Stop being ridiculous."

"Besides, I'd rather have pancakes than waffles any day of the week, month, or year."

At that moment, I realized that I had underestimated Ivylee's talent for being annoying. Without my realizing it, she had become as insidious as kudzu and about as stifling. "And what stupid meaning is that supposed to have?"

"Oh, nothing," Ivylee answered with her finger between her teeth as she twirled like a toy top winding-down. "Except that waffles are lumpy, not soft and smooth like pancakes. It's like I told my Mr. Robinson when we first met. I said, 'Sister is so lumpy.' Maybe you could use that iron to press out some of your lumps." Ivylee pointed to the iron I had left cooling on the floor by the closet door.

"Why, you lazy, little witch. I'll show you where I'll use that iron." Like a thief snatching a purse, I jerked the plug out of the wall and grabbed the iron while Ivylee took off running around the living room, jumping over furniture and dodging the iron with me attached to the other end of it.

"You better put that thing down before I call Momma."

"Go ahead. Call her, and I'll tell her how you developed such a bad case of poison ivy without ever going near it."

"Oh? Well, I'll tell her all about you and the chicken doctor."

Chalk one up to the ninny. Stoned sober by her comment and the fact that she *knew*, I stopped corpse-still in my tracks. My eyes didn't blink. Nothing moved. I'm not sure I was even breathing.

Ivylee danced around me like she was playing "ring around the rosy," and I was her pocket full of posies, turned red. "Oops. All those times Momma thought you were out there in the chicken house inspecting chickens with the chicken doctor, and all the while, you and him were getting it on underneath the brooders. What's it like to have eighteen thousand beady, little eyes watching you, Sister?"

"Oh, you foul-mouthed swine. For your information, we were putting a splint on a chicken with a bad leg."

"No doubt. Must be kinda dangerous out there for them chickens when y'all get to rolling around, huh? Don't believe I've ever seen so many feathers flying. Tell me, Sister, did the chicken doctor ask you to cackle when you climaxed?"

Before I could pound her to death with the iron, we heard Momma coming. I pointed the iron at Ivylee like it was a spray gun filled with deadly poison. "You say one word."

From the front porch, we overheard Momma as she stopped to converse with the stump and then the familiar knock on the door board casing.

"Anybody there?" When no one answered, Momma came inside. "What do you reckon that sign is doing out there in the yard? I don't remember seeing a sign out there before. So must be a sign for sure."

"No doubt," I agreed as Momma untied the scarf to her straw hat.

"A sign of what?" Grinning big like a crescent moon, Ivylee picked up her paper creation and danced in my direction. "Maybe it's a sign that the chicken doctor's coming."

"Why would a One Way sign be a sign that the chicken doctor's coming? It don't even point to the chicken house." Looking like she might be standing before a chalkboard to test Ivylee's theory, with her head tilted to one side, Momma pondered the suggestion in a sincere effort to evaluate its validity. "Ivylee, maybe you should go lie down for a while, Sweetie. I think the heat might have made you a little dizzy."

Pleased with herself, Ivylee twisted her shoulders back and forth while biting her lower lip. "Whatever you say, Momma, dear. I'll do that very thing as soon as I finish here." Ivylee pranced back to the sofa like she had won first prize at the County Fair. "I'll just finish weaving this section first."

Glaring at Ivylee with all the anger I could muster, I added, "Everything to you is a sign, Momma."

"You think we had another tornado last night?" At once aware of me standing in the middle of the living room holding the iron, Momma looked puzzled. "Sister, what are you doing with the iron?"

"Oh, I, uh, saw this wrinkle on the curtain and thought I'd press it out." As though I had planned this as an important part of my day, I walked over to the window and proceeded to press the curtain.

Momma looked confused like maybe Ivylee and I had switched heads. "Don't you think it would be easier if you took it off the window first?"

"Well, yes," I stuttered, "but I didn't have time for that."

"Why? You got somewhere to go? You not gonna try

and run away again, are you?"

"No, it was too embarrassing having you post a reward for me the last time."

Momma removed the rope of black garland from the sewing basket and measured its length with her arms. "I'm sorry, Sister. I wish we could let you leave, but we need you here. Can't nobody run this farm better than you. But I do wish you'd help me a little more with Precious though."

"Let Ivylee help you with Precious."

Momma draped the black garland across the window and stepped back to admire her handiwork, as it looped over and against the white curtain. It looked as though we were getting an early start decorating for Halloween, but then when memorial services for an amputated leg are a routine part of your day, no doubt you are always ready for Halloween. "Why black garland?" I asked once. As though answering a question from the Primary Class at Sunday School, Momma responded, "Well, it shows up better against white, and everybody knows black and white go with everything."

While I wrapped the electrical cord around the iron, Momma reminded, "And you know Ivylee is prone to sun strokes, Sister."

"The only thing Ivylee is prone to is not working. And you don't need to get over-heated. You'll have another spell with your heart. Do you have your pills in your pocket?"

Momma removed a small, brown bottle of Nitroglycerin from her apron pocket to show me.

Without looking up from her paper contraption, Ivylee added, "That's right, Momma. The last time you had a spell on us, you went the color of Bunk's leg, and I don't have any shade of blush to fix that, especially since the Avon lady may not be coming back after you had her paint the toenails on Bunk's leg."

Momma removed the rock from her apron pocket, placed it against her ear like it was a seashell in which she might hear the sounds of the ocean and listened with rapt intensity. When apparently nothing spoke to her, she placed the rock inside the coffin. "Sure is hot today. We could use some rain to wash down all this dust."

One of Ivylee's few chores is to dust, which she doesn't do, but she actually does have a chore, other than just being one. With her memory spurred, Momma asked, "Did you remember to dust the furniture, Ivylee?"

"Why, no, Momma, not yet. You see, I was working on this poem, but Sister here interrupted me."

"You couldn't write an epitaph for an atheist on a good day, Ivylee."

Ivylee stuck her tongue out at me and sashayed across the room. I did not trust the little twit any more than I would a jackal to baby sit chickens, so I paused for whatever newest nonsense she had devised.

Having lived with Momma and Ivylee all these years, I like to think I have been prepared for most circumstances that could arise, especially those that leave a person speechless, like all of a sudden seeing a total stranger naked. I must say though that even with my vast experience, I was ill-prepared for what came next.

With the white, paper contraption that she had been working on for months in her hands, Ivylee opened the oven door, climbed on top of the stove, and placed the paper creation onto her shoulders. "'Paper Angels' by Ivylee. 'In my aloneness, I make angels. Paper angels cannot fly, make no music from their 'O's.' The 'O' in the mirror is not mine, as I check to see if I am there. I am not—gone long this time. Paper angels cannot fly. Sticks and stones and broken bones, but words cannot help me.

Paper angels cannot fly, cannot sit upon a shoulder high.
Paper, scissors, rock—paper loses every time, cannot win,
only mock. Paper angels cannot fly, and no longer can I.'"

After this recitation of her most recent paper and
"poetica" creation, Ivylee, like some paper-winged creature
from an endangered tree, spread her wings as though she
were about to fly right off the top of that stove and into the
air. Like a backwards bee trying to land on a flower, Ivylee
fluttered those paper wings in the air before bringing them
together in front of her in an attempt to hide her torso. The
effect of this spectacle was probably akin to the experience
of a drug-induced hallucination, and I wondered what ring
Dante would have assigned it.

Pleased as a pea-picker standing before an empty pea
field, Momma stood and applauded. "That was lovely, dear.
The best one yet. Wasn't that just too much, Sister?"

"Oh, it was definitely too much all right. It always is."

After Ivylee completed reveling in her winged stovetop
accomplishments, she sat down on the door of the oven to
admire her paper creation.

As Momma walked across the room to the screen door,
she paused long enough to pat Ivylee on top of the head
like she was a puppy.

"Precious, get out of that pond. You gonna slide down
and drown. Oh, I hope he doesn't try to baptize Ernestine's
cat again. You know, sometimes he don't act right."

"Precious has never acted right, not since. . ." I stopped
abruptly as I realized what would follow was going to open
a door I did not want open. "Sorry, Momma, I won't bring
it up again."

"If we could all spend a little more time with him.
Ivylee, why don't you share some of your poetry with him?
He would love it, I'm sure, and it might even inspire you.
Precious is always reciting stuff to me. Of course I don't

understand most of it, but I act like I do, and it seems to make him happy."

Waving her paper wings like she might join the covey of empty-eyed birds hanging from the ceiling, Ivylee floated across the room as she whooshed away Momma's suggestion. "I don't need Precious to inspire my poetry. My Mr. Robinson provides me with all the inspiration I need."

"In the form of a cucumber maybe."

"I only like cucumbers in sandwiches, but then I've never 'cackled' about it." Ivylee looked at me and grinned as if a warming sensation may have dispersed itself throughout her body and into her empty head.

If I had a strong enough piece of string, I would have been all too pleased to hang her from the ceiling with all the other artificial birds. "I got it! Maybe Ivylee could get a job in town writing death notices for the *Joy Examiner*."

"Ivylee's got too much talent to bury it in the obituaries, Sister."

"She's apparently got too much talent to do any kind of work, even chores." I removed a dust cloth from the closet and proceeded to do what I do every day, Ivylee's chores.

Momma had assumed her seat on the sofa and stroked the coffin like it was a bottle with a genie that had long eluded her. "Oh, I wish Bunk were here. He always knew what to say whenever I got a touch of the melancholy. Maybe he'll be here tomorrow. I know he'll want to come back for his leg. Don't you think he will?"

The white, paper-winged, parrot mimicked, "I'm sure he will, Momma."

While I watered the wilting flowers, Momma removed the rock from her pocket and placed it inside the coffin. From her sewing and craft basket, Momma removed a pair of scissors, crossed to the screen door, and trimmed the cotton I had placed in the hole in the screen earlier.

Standing at the door, she studied the sky like it held some answer or assurance for her. "Looks like a thunderhead's a-brewing. Hope no more stuff lands in the yard. Peculiar the way it does that. First, that stone, then that stump and now this sign. Makes it awful confusing."

"Momma, why don't you let Harley haul it all off?"

"Goodness, no. I can't do that. Might be a sign."

"A sign we're insane maybe."

Momma's attention was turned to something in the distance. "Precious, Honey, what have you got there? That a bird? Not a robin, is it? Be careful. Don't squeeze too hard. You might make its eyes pop out. Sister, go out there and see if you can get him to let that robin go. Wouldn't look right for Precious to be out there popping the eyes out of robins with us living here at 'Robin's Rest.'"

"Momma, this is not 'Robin's Rest.' Just because you let Leon go and paint 'Robin's Rest' on the side of the barn, don't make it so. People think we're crazy doing stuff like that. Besides, we never see any robins around here anyway. All we see are chickens."

"And the chicken doctor, he sees lots of chickens and one old crow," Ivylee smirked.

"But at least he doesn't have poison ivy."

Momma looked confused for a moment. "You're not looking in the right place, Sister. And that's not true. I have you know I saw a robin the day Ivylee got sick and the day Bunk disappeared and the day Precious got into the chicken house." After I finished dusting the sideboard, Momma removed a table runner from one of the drawers and placed it on top of the sideboard.

"That's all the same day, Momma."

Undaunted by fact or reality, Momma added, "You know, sometimes I wonder if Bunk weren't following a robin the day he disappeared. He always said that if you spot a robin, you'll know."

The cuckoo bird with the paper wings turned her attention to this comment. "I always wondered about that, Momma. What is it exactly that you'll know?"

"Well, I don't rightly know, but Bunk always knew, so I figure one day, I'll know too. I just hope I know that I know."

"I hope that you know that you know too, Momma," Ivylee offered.

Having heard this conversation enough times to sprout feathers myself, I intentionally redirected it by holding up one of the baskets of funeral flowers in front of Momma. "Can I throw these out now? They've bitten the dust and served their last service."

"Not until I can get some fresh ones out of the cemetery. I'll make a note of it, Sister, and thank you for reminding me. And, Ivylee, while I'm getting us some fresh flowers, why don't you go spend a little time with Precious? He would love to hear some of your poetry. You could put your wings on and perform on the front porch."

"There's nothing out there, Momma."

"Empty head, empty eyes," I chimed.

"You're just trying to make me sound stupid. Well, I'm not going to fall for it. When my Mr. Robinson comes and whisks me away to our beautiful home in Miami. . ."

Like a cat on a wharf rat, I pounced on the paper-bird-woman of the robinless Robin's Rest. "Yes, and Precious out there will be seated at the right hand of God."

"Don't be sacrilegious, Sister. You'll burn in hell. Oh, that reminds me, I better go check the meat loaf."

As Momma toddled out of the room, she sang, ". . .I'll fly away, old glory, I'll fly away. When I die, hallelujah, by and by, I'll fly away."

And secretly, I prayed I could.

Chapter 7

Bunk

When Bunk left, it was a death of sorts, the near death of a family and a life, as we had known it. We never grew accustomed to the pain; we merely grew accustomed to its presence. For me, Bunk's departure had come to be managed pain—I managed by keeping busy, by working so hard that it was pushed aside during the day, and I could count on exhaustion to take over at night. This worked for me, most of the time.

Momma managed her pain by the use of make believe. Momma was Bunk's life support, and he was hers, and she would hold on to him by whatever means possible, whether that be through memorial services for an amputated leg or as the Precious pet that ruled the family roost.

Although I tried not to remember or to think about it, I missed the Bunk of my childhood. As a daddy, he was a quiet man, who for the most part did not interact a great deal with his children, but we never doubted his love. Our daddy's love for us was simply a quiet love.

Once when I was a teenager, we piled into the old Biscayne Chevrolet and traveled to the city to have Sunday dinner with some distant relatives. Elvis was king, and his movie "Blue Hawaii" had recently been released. Although Ivylee and I did not get to go to the movies often when we were growing up, Momma and Bunk allowed us to go with the older sister of a friend to see Elvis's first movie after he was released from the Army. It was a big deal to us.

One member of the family we were visiting that Sunday afternoon was an older cousin, who for some reason, simply did not care for me. While she tolerated Ivylee, and at times even seemed to like her, something about me rubbed her the wrong way, which, given my sweet nature, was hard to understand. Although I could not appreciate this at the time, I do now. There are some people in life you just don't like, regardless of the circumstances or even if they are related. Relativity does not necessarily assure appreciation.

Encouraged by her mother, my cousin took Ivylee and me to her room where she showed us her newly acquired copy of Elvis's "Blue Hawaii" album. When we told her that we had seen the movie, she became so indignant at the idea that her country bumpkin cousins had also seen it, she announced, "Well, I have seen it too, and I'm probably going to go see it again, and I have the album." And she was right about that. She did have the album, and I stood before her, coveting it like a hungry child. Life on a farm does not allow for much beyond the essentials. Any monies earned, for the most part, go toward food and clothing. While it may be a good life, it is often a simple one out of necessity.

The next day when we came home from school, I went to my room to deposit my books and there laying in the center of my bed was a "Blue Hawaii" album. I was stunned like perhaps I had come home to the wrong house. When I mentioned it to Momma, she said, "Bunk got it for you." I was so taken aback I didn't know how to respond at first. I was not aware that he had overheard any of that Sunday conversation. On his breakfast plate the next morning, I placed a royal blue morning glory, his favorite flower. He never mentioned the album.

Before Bunk took up residence in the tool shed, Momma cleaned and decorated Bunk's new living quarters. The theme for these new quarters was rainbows, and with the exception of having Ivylee make paper rainbows to hang around the room, Momma did all the work herself. She neither asked nor would have allowed us to help. Bunk was hers, and whatever happened between them was also hers.

On the wall, behind the headboard of Bunk's bed, Momma painted a huge rainbow. On each side of the bed, at each end of the rainbow were two little white tables. On top of one table was Bunk's Bible and a lamp, and on top of the other one was a family photograph of the four of us at an earlier time. One of the chairs from the kitchen table sat beside the bed. Momma ordered rainbow sheets and a little rainbow rug from the Spiegel catalog, and she bought an old chiffarobe from one of the neighbors for Bunk's clothes. A small gas heater sat at one end of the shed with a rocking chair in front of it. Only Momma or I could light the heater, as Bunk was no longer allowed to have matches.

The day Bunk set fire to the living room, he had been helping Momma shell some chestnuts. Actually, he watched while Momma removed the shells as she chattered on to him about first one thing and then another. He seemed to be more attentive than usual that day, and I remember being surprised by this as I watched the two of them. When

Momma finished removing the shell and husk of the last chestnut, she stood and said, "Now let me go get some freezer bags for these." His eyes watched her leave the room, and he stared at the door where she had disappeared. I had finished folding a load of towels and went to put them away.

What happened next is still something of a mystery, but I heard Momma screaming and saw smoke coming from the living room. Although the fire was a small one, it was enough to scare us. When I entered, Momma was swatting the burning paper bag of shells and husks with a hand towel.

"Stop, Momma! You're fanning the fire!"

Ivylee came running out of her room to watch. "Sister, do something!"

"Momma, go get a bucket of water!" When I looked about the room, the afghan on the back of the sofa was all that was available to try to smother the fire. I grabbed it and tossed it on the burning bag, which by this time had ignited the rug around it. "Ivylee, get me a blanket or something!"

Momma ran in with a dishpan full of water, which she tossed onto the fire and me. "Momma, do I look like I'm on fire? Go get another pan of water!"

Like an awkward antelope, Ivylee came running in and tossed a quilt over the fire and me. Grappling with the quilt, I stood and gently laid it across the fire. "What in blazes is wrong with the two of you?"

Momma poured the second pan of water onto the smoldering fire and quilt while I fumed. "Lord, I hope I'm never caught in a dangerous situation with y'all. My chances of surviving would be significantly lessened. And what took you so long to get the quilt, Ivylee?"

"Well, I had to figure out which one was the oldest. I knew Momma wouldn't want me burning up one of her good quilts."

"Ivylee, the house was on fire. If the house burns, there would be no quilts to concern yourself about." When I stopped fussing long enough to look at Momma, she was as white as a cloud and about as far away. "Momma, I'll clean up. Why don't you go lie down for a little while?" Then I realized Momma's wide-open eyes were on Bunk, who stood in a corner holding a box of matches. His eyes were dull again, and he looked like he was back behind a translucent scrim that only he could see.

"He set the fire!" Ivylee yelled. "I'm not living under the same roof with him. He's crazy, and he's dangerous."

"Shut-up, Ivylee." Momma had tears in her eyes, but she didn't cry. She took the matches away from him and led him outside. On the steps of the front porch, I watched while she placed his head on her shoulder, and she rocked and sang to him for several hours. Whether she told him she was moving him to the tool shed that day or not, I don't know, but whatever she said, somewhere in her words, the two of them found peace with it.

The house reeked of smoke for weeks, and it took several days of cleaning to get the smoky film off everything. The rug had to be thrown away, and the wooden floor beneath wasn't scarred too badly. We moved the sofa to cover the scar and did without a rug until we could afford another one.

We never spoke of the fire again, and neither of us challenged Momma when Bunk was moved out of the house. If he objected, we never knew it. If anything, from that time on, he seemed to be frightened of the house.

On the day we moved Bunk to the tool shed, he looked confused and older than I ever recalled seeing him. Momma took him by the hand and led him around the room, showing and explaining every detail in a reassuring voice. He looked and listened, but did not appear to take any of it in. That night I watched as she helped him get ready for bed. The two of them said nothing to each other as she helped him into his pajamas. When Momma said his prayers for him, for a moment, I thought I saw a tear run down his cheek. She turned off the lamp, sat in the chair beside his bed, and held his hand until he fell asleep. I waited outside the door for her, and when she came out, her eyes were strained and glistening in the porch light. When I asked if Bunk was okay, she simply said, "Bunk's gone, and now we have Precious." She turned and tottered toward the house, and the next day, Precious roamed the yard like an apparition, a shadow of what was, and Momma worried and doted over him like the child he had become to her.

All of Bunk's meals included at least one favorite food, and she baked teacakes for him at least once a week. Each day, she squeezed half-a-dozen lemons so that he would have lemonade. Once a week, Momma prepared a picnic lunch for the two of them, and they often ate tomato sandwiches as they sat on a handmade quilt down near the pond.

One day I observed their picnic from the front porch where I was enjoying one of Momma's fried chocolate pies. While Momma jabbered on and on about church, the garden, the girls, Precious counted the squares of fabric on the quilt. I wondered if he saw memories in those pieces of fabric, as I did when I looked at them—a dress my grandmother had worn, an old apron of Momma's, a skirt Ivylee and I had both worn in first grade, my childhood flannel pajamas. If he did recall those memories, he kept them to himself.

Precious talked; he just didn't talk to us, not that we could have understood what he was saying even if he had talked to us. Most of what he said didn't make any sense.

Trying to understand it was like listening to multiple conversations of different people happening at the same time, but from one person. Regardless, whatever he said, Momma listened, smiled, and agreed. And just like with Ivylee, she encouraged him to find himself.

During all that time, not once did Momma ever completely abandon Bunk. At the onset of Bunk's amnesia, Dr. Nettles had explained that the amnesia could leave as suddenly as it had appeared, and Momma held on to those words and that hope like they were her inner tube in the river that now flooded our lives. Although the flood had hit hard at first, it eventually settled into a continuous flow.

One spring, Momma and Precious made Easter bunnies out of wash clothes. There wasn't a single wash cloth in the house safe from being rolled, tied, and tortured into the shape of a square-looking rabbit. And everywhere you looked, some washcloth bunny would pop up. I opened my underwear drawer one morning to find a pink, eyeless bunny nesting there among my cotton undies. A funny thing about his bunnies though was that none of them had eyes, and if Momma glued eyes on them, Precious would take them off.

Soon we had so many bunnies that Momma began looking for other uses or homes for them. Several had been taken to the cemetery where they perched upon funeral flower sprays in the same location that an artificial dove once nested. But the most embarrassing bunny appearance had to be when Momma put a green one in the offering plate at church one Sunday morning.

Most people at our church had the good manners not to mention it to me, except for Aunt Maisy, who could lay claim to good manners only when it suited her, but when it came to holding her tongue, she had no manners and no tact whatsoever. Aunt Maisy lived in a large, white Taralooking house on the edge of town. Being centrally located, it was easier for her to keep up with everybody else's business. Everybody called her Aunt Maisy, although to my knowledge, she had no living relatives, probably because she had worried them all to death. Her father had been a judge, which might explain why Aunt Maisy decided that that was her calling in life, to sit in judgment of everybody else. Rumor had it that she had been over-indulged as a child—a condition she apparently never outgrew.

Aunt Maisy had appointed herself the town's conscience, and when something did not suit her, she felt obliged to share her opinion about it, whether it involved her or not. She often helped out at the church and did as much as everybody would let her do, including dictate the preacher's sermons, if she felt a particular one was needed.

The Sunday Momma placed the green bunny in the offering plate, Aunt Maisy marched up to me after the service like a sergeant on a mission. "Exactly what does your momma think we can do with that bunny rabbit?" she demanded. "Put it in the envelope to pay the electric bill? And it don't even have any eyes."

Not being the sort of person who lets too much slide, I felt it my duty to offer some suggestions for the use of Momma's bunny, although my surroundings prevented me from suggesting the best use for it.

After I stepped my smart-mouth self right up and into Aunt Maisy's face, I explained with enough indignation and disapproval to mount a full-scale skirmish over the matter, "Maybe she thought Pastor Mike could *heal* it. Or maybe she thought he could possibly use that washcloth to wash away some folks' sins."

Standing nearby, Pastor Mike overheard the conversation and had the good judgment to intervene before I took that goofy-looking, avocado-green hat Aunt

Maisy was wearing and fashioned it into a sliver of a belt around her unpleasantly plump middle. "It's quite all right, Miss Maisy. We're going to use it as a model for the children to make bunnies during Bible School this year." Pastor Mike quickly escorted her to her car, and Aunt Maisy lived to bring pain another day.

After Vacation Bible School that summer, washcloth bunny rabbits showed up all over town. Sheriff Dorsey even had one sitting up in the back window of his patrol car. Apparently, they had been healed, as they all had eyes.

On more than one occasion, we had been the source of a sermon or two at our church and probably at the church on the other end of town as well. One particular sermon, entitled "Reverence for The Sanctuary of the Dead," was no doubt inspired by some of Momma's excursions to the cemetery. Momma would sometimes take Precious with her on a graveyard trip, as much to give him a change of scenery as anything. One afternoon while Momma was working in the garden, Precious slipped off to the cemetery by himself. For some strange reason, he decided to relocate several of the smaller gravestones. When he finished, the cemetery looked like a kind of distorted miniature Stonehenge. Momma and I tried to put all the gravestones back in the right place, and her memory served us as best it could in this regard, but who besides Momma would commit grave locations to memory outside their own kin? The ordeal of trying to relocate the gravestones to their rightful place was like playing some weird Tales-from-the-Crypt memory game.

At our church, Mother's Day, Homecoming, and Memorial Day occur and are celebrated on the same day. People come from all over to visit the final resting place of their loved one and to decorate their loved one's grave. The Memorial Sunday following the gravestone switch was unlike any other I have experienced. Some folks wandered around all afternoon looking a tad bewildered by the location of their relative's grave. I stayed off to the side and tried to look as innocent as a guilt-ridden person can look, while Momma wandered from person to person exclaiming, "I'll declare, we have had the worst tornado season this year than I ever recall, and the most peculiar things have been happening."

People would smile and nod, but when she walked away, their eyes would follow her with skepticism, as if she had told them Martians had landed on the church steeple. All in all, most of the relocations were not far from their original site, but by far the worst oversight was the grave marker of a seventy-eight year old man that now marked an infant's grave. There just didn't seem to be any way to justify it, not even with a tornado, and people looked at Momma with more suspicion than usual for the rest of the day.

Precious was no longer allowed to go to the cemetery, but Momma found other ways to entertain him. One spring, she tried to get him to help her plant the garden, and for about an hour, all was going well, until Precious became distracted and took off behind the plow and plowed a row right through the middle of the front yard. But Momma never gave up. Every morning, she would prepare Precious' breakfast, write "I love YOU" on a piece of paper and place it all on a wooden tray. I often helped by tagging along to open doors. With a smile, she would enter his room and say, "Good morning, baby, and how are we doing this morning? Ready to have a big breakfast? Looks like it's going to be another beautiful day. And what would my Precious like to do today?"

One morning as I was coming out of the chicken house, I stopped and watched the two of them weave morning glory vines into flower garlands and place them on top of each other's head. Momma paused and looked into Precious' eyes for a long time, like if she looked long enough, she might see some inkling of Bunk somewhere in there. When Momma said nothing or offered no direction to him, Precious reached up and picked one of the bright blue flowers from the garland on top of her head and handed it to her. Momma took the flower and stuffed the end of it into the top buttonhole of her sweater. Like someone smitten, she leaned forward and kissed him on the cheek. She wore the morning glory the rest of the day, even after it had long since closed, and that evening, I saw her press it to her lips and place it inside her Bible.

When Bunk was moved out of the house, he became Precious, because that's what he was to Momma and always would be. Bunk, as Momma had known him was gone, gone somewhere far away, but would hopefully one day find his way back home.

Chapter 8

What's Real

On a hot July morning, I stood on the front porch and removed the coveralls I wore to work in the chicken house. As I hung the coveralls on a wooden peg by the screen door, I could hear Momma in the living room reading what sounded like recipes.

In a chicken house filled with full-grown chickens, dust is such a constant condition that some days the air is like a dirty cloud floating above the chickens, pinned in by the roof and walls. Chickens can fly only a few feet, but create enough dust that the atmosphere becomes a chicken house dust storm. The smell of excrement is strong, pungent, acrid and burns the nostrils, and the dust lands everywhere, on every thing, even eyelashes.

On this rain-denied July morning, the dust had been particularly bad. After I removed my shoes and the bandana tied around my head, I brushed my hair back and forth many times with my hands to brush out the remaining dust.

From a nail on one of the well house posts, I removed an old dishpan, filled it with a bucket of water drawn from the well and washed my face and hands. Dust-free enough to enter the house, I found Momma sitting in the middle of the sofa with an open cookbook in her lap.

"Oh, Sister, it's you. I thought I heard a knock and feared it might be God come to bring me another rock, but I haven't even figured out what to do with this one yet." Momma marveled at the rock, turning it from side-to-side like a prize egg with some wondrous treasure inside.

The morning was long and hot, and I was in no mood to cater to Momma's make believe. Thinking the message tied around the rock was from "Doc," I had waited with my heart all a-twitter for the chicken doctor, who never came. Although I wasn't sure what this meant, I knew enough to know it wasn't good. While "Doc" and I had known each other for a long time, we had only recently become involved. I didn't know if what I felt for this man was love, lust, or merely a desire to escape my life's circumstances.

Unbeknown to Momma and Ivylee, one evening while I was alone in the chicken house, preparing medicine to give to the chickens, the reality, the loneliness of my life overwhelmed me, and as I waited for the barrels to fill with water to add the medicine, I considered climbing inside the barrel and sitting there until the water drowned out whatever measly semblance of life I claimed. The doorstop on these thoughts was my spiritual beliefs—if I had learned but one thing from all the church services and religious instruction in my life, it was that suicide was the unforgivable sin.

"How had my life come to this," I wondered. "When did youthful hope and promise succumb to drudgery and obligation?" I knew the answers. I just couldn't justify the fairness of it. I had not been exceedingly bad or particularly good. I was simply a person trying to get on in this world, trying to fulfill whatever plan or promise that had been outlined for me, assuming that one had. I had no delusions of being rich or famous, finding a cure for anything or leading the way to world peace. I wanted to be a forest ranger, to plant myself in nature somewhere in the beautiful Blue Ridge Mountains, where I believed I might find my purpose.

There on the platform that held the two barrels filled with medicine diluted with water for sickly chickens, I broke down and cried, sobbed so heavily that my body shook, because I saw no solutions and acknowledged that apparently, I had little or no purpose. At my lowest point, I knelt down among the chickens and prayed with more sincerity than I had ever prayed. Moments later when I stood up, to my surprise, Doc was standing behind me. Along with my self-pity, the timing of his presence suggested in my beleaguered mind a response to my prayers that in my weakness I accepted not out of love or even desire, but as a distraction from what was going on or not going on in my life. "Was he the answer," my weary mind considered. At the time, it seemed an easy enough thought to believe and justify. I had prayed, and he was there, so he must be the answer. I was defeated enough to accept this as a response to my prayers, as convoluted or irrational as that may sound. When he asked if I was all right, I shook my head and closed my eyes, and I allowed him to comfort me, which he did many times.

Comfort may not be the same as love, but it was better than nothing, and nothing was all I had. I was naïve or stupid enough to believe that no one would ever know, and if no one knew, no one would be hurt. The deceptions we feed ourselves to justify and avoid any unpleasant truths about our behavior.

This morning, the fact that Doc was most likely done with me was hitting pretty hard. Facing that fact as well as myself was bearing down on me also. As I listened to Momma read her recipes, I closed my eyes and took in a deep breath. While I tried to redirect the thoughts that were plaguing my mind, I braced myself for another day like yesterday and the day before.

"Sister, are you all right? You look a little peaked."

"I'm just tired, Momma."

"I'm sorry, dear. Are you not sleeping well? That will sure make you tired. Would you like for us to turn your mattress today? Might help you sleep better."

"I'm fine, Momma."

"Did you get the chickens fed?" Momma pushed the cookbook in my direction.

"Fed, watered, medicated, and ventilated, and yes, I bolted the door behind me."

"That's nice. Now maybe you could help me find a recipe, if you don't mind."

"A recipe for what?"

"Thought I'd make Bunk some rock candy. The Bible says, '. . .upon this rock, I will build. . ..'" Momma stopped and studied the rock as she tried to recall. "I will build something."

"Don't think they were talking about rock candy, Momma. Besides, Bunk is not here. Remember?"

"But you never know when he might come back. Why, I expect he'll be along any day now to collect his leg."

"Whatever for? Exactly what do you think he's going to do with the leg? Hang it on a chain and wear it around his neck?" I looked at Momma whose greatest challenge of the day was finding a candy recipe for the lost warrior who wandered our yard fighting whatever demons chased him, and I felt my resentment for her mount like buzzards in flight toward a recent kill.

"Well, I would imagine it would be an awful nuisance having that thing hanging around your neck. How would a body ever get anything done?"

"The leg is dead, dead and useless, Momma. It can't do Bunk any good now. It can't do anybody any good now. You can memorialize it, serve it, preserve it, and pray over it, but it won't do any good. It's still a dead leg. And the best thing to do with a dead leg is to bury it."

"It's what's in your heart, Sister," Momma explained, sounding like my first-grade Sunday School teacher.

"The heart is a deceiver, Momma, and if you listen to it, it'll make a fool of you every time."

"The Bible says never call anybody a fool."

"The Bible is a book! It is not life! It doesn't eat and drink and sleep and wake. It doesn't wait day-after-day and wonder night-after-night. It lies solitary, still, silent, depending on nothing or no one, and none of it matters to a book."

Perplexed, Momma looked at me as though she thought I had stumped my toe. "Did you step in some ca-ca out in the chicken house?"

"It is not ca-ca. It is dung, and that's all it is! Wading through dung in nothing but nylons."

"You been wearing your good nylons in the chicken house? What ever will you wear to the service if you wear your good nylons to the chicken house?"

My mind released a sigh that seemed to travel all the way through my body to finally escape through my mouth. "I don't want to do the service anymore, Momma. Can't you understand? We've done the service long enough. Let's bury the leg."

Momma stared at me as though I had committed some illogical sacrilege. "We can't bury Bunk's leg. Not with

Bunk still alive. It might bring him all sorts of bad luck."

"Seems to me Bunk's already had his share of bad luck. How about if we bury it with a rabbit's foot? Maybe any bad luck would be cancelled out by good luck. Either that or they could resurrect as the Easter bunny from Hades, hoppity-hobbling, one-legged along, hiding rotten Easter eggs all around the world for fools to find."

Confusion crossed Momma's face like she had stepped inside the wrong waiting room. She closed the cookbook and placed it inside the coffin. "Sister, you're starting to make less sense to me than Ivylee, and that scares me. Why don't we give you a laxative on Monday? Start your week off right."

I stood at the screen door staring at nothing and looked about our lives. My heart fell to the floor, and if I could have, I would have stepped on it like the black widow spider that it was. I could feel defeat blanket me once again as I succumbed to Momma's arranged world. "A laxative cannot cure life."

"I don't know. Sometimes a good purge can give you a whole new perspective."

"From an outhouse maybe. Not from the grave." Like the mechanical moron I had become, I removed the broom from the front porch and swept the living room.

"We talking about the leg again? We can't bury Bunk's leg. We got to live up to our obligations."

"Obligations rob you, Momma."

"Family's all we got, Honey, and we have to cling to it like ivy to a tree."

"Poison ivy maybe."

"Look, Sweetie. Try not to think about it. Try to put it in one of those forgetting places, and leave it there."

"One of those forgetting places?" I clutched the handle of the broom in my hands like it was the bar of a jungle gym I was desperately trying to hang onto to keep from dropping into the mire. "Momma, I *live* in one of those forgotten places."

"It'll get better. I'm sure it will. Just try to pretend. It'll make it not seem so bad. Remember what the song says?" Momma removed the broom from my grip, leaned it against the wall and took both my hands in hers as she tried to get me to dance. "'Just let the sun shine in, Face it with a grin. Just open up your heart, and let the sun shine in. . . .' What's that other part? Something, something '. . .frowners never win.'"

"I didn't realize it was a contest."

"Why, all life is a contest, Honey. There's the winners, and there's the losers, and we want to be winners."

"How can you tell the difference?"

With sweet awareness, Momma smiled like she had received the secret of life and was about to share it with me. "The winners are always happy." Turning her attention to the outdoors, she asked, "By the way, what was Precious doing when you came in?"

"Sleeping under the porch."

"Ain't that sweet?"

"And I suppose Precious is a winner?"

"Well, he's happy, ain't he?"

"Momma, Precious is. . ."

Before I could complete the sentence, Momma interrupted, "I know what Precious is."

With all the intensity my eyes could express, I ventured, "Do you, Momma? Do you really know anymore?"

"I know he's all I got of what was." The dance stopped. "What is this all about, Sister?" Momma read my mood like it was a road map to the foundation of this conversation. "Look, we're getting a new chicken doctor. I already put in for a new one last week."

Shocked to my core, I pulled back from Momma like she was contagious. "How did you know? Ivylee told you! The little snitch." As angry with Ivylee as I have ever been, I marched to the door that led to the hall and yelled with as much breath as my lungs could muster. "Ivylee, get you blabbermouth self in here right now."

"Now don't go and get yourself all riled up. Ivylee didn't tell me. It was his wife. She told me."

"She did not. She didn't know."

"She most certainly did know. Said it was all them feathers in his underwear, and she wasn't none too nice about it either. Said she was going to shoot you. And I told her I didn't think that would be a very Christian thing to do. I was afraid she might blow your leg off. And you know what a nuisance that would be. Why, you liable to topple over out in the chicken house, and them chickens might peck your eyes out. How would you ever get around with an artificial leg and no eyes? So that's when I decided the best thing to do was to put in for a new chicken doctor. And they're sending us one, all the way from Heard County. Imagine that."

"Oh, Momma." I sunk down into the over-stuffed chair like it was quagmire sucking me into its depths, and I could feel myself going under.

"When I told his wife that, she agreed not to shoot you. Of course, we ain't heard from the new chicken doctor yet, but I'm sure we will any day now."

"He was all I had, Momma."

"You didn't have him, Honey. He belonged to somebody else, and somebody that belongs to somebody else is nothing but a bounder."

"A bounder?"

"Yes, a bounder." Momma sat on top of the coffin in front of me and took both my hands in hers. "Bound to hurt you and bound to leave you with nothing but a broken-heart. And that's not true, Honey. He's not all you got. You got me and Ivylee, and Precious out there thinks the sun rises and sets in you."

"No, I got nothing, Momma. The chicken doctor was real."

"What we do every day of our life is real. The rest don't matter."

"Maybe not to you." Hopelessness overcame me like a heavy wool blanket, and whatever strength I possessed seemed to ooze out my pores. "Without the rest, life is a death sentence, a daily death sentence that grows more demanding every day."

"Enough of this kind of talk. It'll just make you sad." Momma stood and picked up one of the baskets of flowers. "Why don't you go with me to get some fresh flowers? The cemetery's pretty this time of day, and flowers can lift your spirit like a little bluebird taking flight."

I stared at Momma like I didn't know her, when in truth, I knew her all too well. When I did not respond, she added as she moved toward the screen door with her basket of wilted flowers, "All I can say is that it's a good thing our chickens haven't been sick."

"And that's about all I would expect you to say." Like a beaten birddog, I walked ahead of her out the front door to I didn't care where.

As I trudged away, I could feel the frantic in Momma's voice try to grasp and hang onto me as she followed. "Try not to take it so hard, Sister. It'll be all right. You'll see. You can inspect chickens with this other chicken doctor. Just you wait."

I left the porch, the house, the yard and tried to close my ears to words I'd heard before and to feelings of the deathwatch inside myself.

Chapter 9

What's Not

Later that day, I sat beside the pond for a long time as I considered what might have been, as opposed to what was. Every now and then, I would cast my fishing line into the water and watch what few fish were in the pond play with the bobble. I did not consider myself a fisherman, but enjoyed the peacefulness of the pond, and the act of casting a line. Like a worm squirming on a hook at the end of a nylon string, I could cast those writhing cares into the water and watch them sink to the bottom to lay deeply submersed among the other bottom dwellers. If I accidentally caught something, I threw it back.

From where I sat, I could see the tool shed where Precious slept. Small paper angels hung from the frame of every windowpane, and I wondered if Precious saw them, was even aware of them.

One morning while I was feeding the chickens, Precious wandered into the chicken house. He had not been anywhere near the chicken house for years. When he stepped inside the door, he looked confused like he had made a wrong turn. The chickens seemed to frighten him, and his eyes were wild with alarm. He had not spoken for a long time, and when I asked, "Are you okay," I didn't expect an answer. With confusion across his face and pleading in his voice, he replied, "He baptized in the name of the Father, the Son and the Holy Ghost. The Ghost won't let me come back." I had no idea what this meant, and I wondered if he did either, but for one brief moment, I thought he may have known who I was, but when I walked toward him, he shook his head, and with a face full of fear, he turned and shuffled away. As I watched him leave, stepping awkwardly over the threshold of the door, I understood for that moment why Momma would not put him away.

In the afternoon of this same day, as I sat in one of the wooden rocking chairs on the front porch, I overheard Momma and Ivylee. From where I sat, I watched through the screened window as Ivylee maneuvered across the room to the overstuffed chair, her favorite roost. She had apparently taken a bath as she wore her tattered blue bathrobe and a towel wrapped about her head. In this get-up, she looked like the southern version of a swami and only needed a crystal ball to make the picture complete.

When Ivylee entered the living room, Momma had been jabbering away to herself about our earlier discussion. If she did not know the loss of the chicken doctor had been a major blow to me, she surely sensed it.

"What's that, Momma?" Ivylee removed a cardboard funeral home fan from underneath the cushion of the overstuffed chair before she plopped down like a kid onto a pile of freshly picked cotton. She fanned herself with one hand and held the other one in mid-air as if to balance herself lest she be blown away by her own hand.

"Oh, I was just talking to Sister."

Ivylee looked around the room. "But Sister's not here."

"She went for a walk."

"In this heat? Surely you must be joshing. Sister spends way too much time out there, and I think it's starting to affect her mind."

Momma removed the dustpan from the closet, and with the broom, swept the pile of dust I had swept earlier onto the pan. "She's not happy, Ivylee."

"And whose fault is that?"

"We got to do something to make her happy."

"The only thing that makes her happy is making us miserable."

Momma looked at the dust in the dustpan like she was trying to figure out what it was doing there. "That's not true, dear. Sister's just not as good at hiding her feelings as we are."

"Well, you're certainly right about that."

"Sister has to work so hard, and I think she sometimes forgets to be nice."

"Well, what else has she got to do?"

"'From dust-to-dust,'" Momma muttered as she opened the oven door of the old stove, pulled out a small basket, dumped the dust into it and closed the oven door. "That's it, Ivylee. Sister needs something. Maybe we could find her a talent." As she stood with one arm across her middle and the other one propped on it, Momma patted her face with her hand to consider the possibilities. When she leaned forward to place the dustpan on the floor inside the closet, the rock fell out of her apron pocket. Momma picked it up, rolled it around in her hand like it was a worry stone, and then snatched it to her bosom as though it had given her the answer. "Maybe we could get her a rock tumbler, and she could tumble rocks. Why, we could decorate the place all purty with all the things Sister could make with her rocks. What do you think, Ivylee?"

"I guess so, Momma. If Sister became an artist like me, maybe she would be more sensitive."

"I bet she would." Delighted with this idea, Momma twirled around once with the broom as though it were her dancing partner for insane ideas.

"But I feel I should warn you, Momma, I have never heard of any artists who are chicken farmers. The two professions do not compliment one another, and she may not be a successful artist."

"I just want her to be happy, Ivylee."

"I know you do, Momma. We all wanna be happy."

Inspired, Momma removed her Bible from inside the coffin. "I read something about that. What was it," she pondered as she thumbed through her Bible. "Oh, here it is. 'Behold we count them happy which endure.'" As though this were the definitive answer to every question, Momma closed her Bible with a snap and returned it to the coffin. "So we must be happy."

"How's that, Momma?"

"Because we endure." With her sewing basket in her lap, Momma cut more paper strips for garland to decorate the living room.

"I don't know about that, Momma. Sometimes it seems like there ought to be more than just getting up and going to bed."

"I know, Honey. We all want more than what we got. Don't you think I want more of Bunk than what I got?" For emphasis, Momma leaned forward and stroked the coffin like it was a cat caressing her legs with its body. "You just have to do the best you can with what you got, and what you got right now is Precious."

"I do not have Precious, Momma. Precious doesn't exist."

"You ought not to be that away, Ivylee. Precious is a cute little bugger, when he ain't acting peculiar. And sometimes, I think he just does all that for attention. Probably lonesome like the rest of us. Why, one day when I went out to water the garden, Precious was laying up under the house counting doodlebugs in the dirt. Ain't that sweet? I used to count doodlebugs in the dirt myself, you know. I remember I'd crawl up under the house and find their little, round holes, and then I'd get a stick and stir that little hole while I recited, 'Doodle bug, doodle bug, your house is on fire. Doodle bug, doodle bug, your house is on fire.' My, that was fun. Did you ever do that, Honey?"

"No, I don't recall as I ever did."

"Well, you should try it sometime. It was loads of fun. Sometimes a dusty, little doodle bug would appear in that hole in the dirt."

"What did you do with it when you found it?"

"Oh, I never did anything with it. I just found it."

"For some reason, Momma, that makes me sad."

"Ain't that odd? Makes me sad too. Wonder why."

With her shoulders sagging like she had taken on the worries of the world, Ivylee stood and placed the fan underneath the cushion. "I don't feel so good, Momma. Think I'll go lie down for a while."

"I'm sorry, Honey, but you shouldn't let yourself get so upset. But then you've always been such a tenderhearted child. A body has to be brave, and like the Bible says, we must endure. Just because something ain't what you want it to be, don't mean it ain't there. And just because something's there, don't mean it's what you want it to be."

At the hall door, Ivylee stopped and turned. "But, Momma. . ."

Momma stood at the screen door, her eyes searching the yard for Precious, when she interrupted Ivylee. "Even if we find life ain't what we intended, don't mean we can stop. The carousel don't stop just because you want to get off. You just gotta keep riding until. . ."

"Until what?" Ivylee asked with a touch of trepidation in her voice.

"Until the dust settles I guess. Enough of this kind of talk. It's lonesome talk that'll only make you feel sad. I tell you what. You go lie down, Honey, while I go hose down Precious. He does so love it when I take the hose to him. Now go on and lie down. A nice nap will make you feel better, you'll see."

"Yes, Momma." Like a wind-up doll, Ivylee turned and left the living room.

From the top step of the porch, Momma searched the yard. "Precious, baby, would you like Momma to come hose you down? I know it's stifling here. Let Momma fix it for you." As Momma descended the steps, she sang part of an old hymn we had often heard at some of the old folks' funerals. "'We're often like the lonesome dove, That mourns her absent mate; From hill to hill, from grove to grove, Her woes she doth relate;. . .'"

I must have turned soft, because I truly felt bad for Ivylee. Maybe because my earlier encounter with Momma had left me feeling hopeless, and I could appreciate her pangs even if I couldn't appreciate her.

When I knocked on Ivylee's door, she didn't answer, but I opened it anyway. "Have you seen Momma?"

"She's hosing down Precious."

"Oh, I must have just missed her. You all right?"

"What do you care?" Ivylee sat up in bed, probably in shock that I had asked. She still had the towel wrapped around her head, still could have passed for a swami, less her crystal ball.

"Oh, I don't know. Guess it seems too hot to be taking a nap." I looked about her room. "When did you change your room around?"

"Over a year ago. You do live here, don't you?"

"I like it this way. You might consider moving your desk over in front of the window though. Give you more sunlight." Ivylee looked at me suspiciously as I stepped into her room.

"Are you about to do something mean to me or play a trick on me?"

"No," I answered. The awkward pause between us was like a huge boulder that we both cautiously peeped around. "If you want me to help you move your desk, I will."

"Why? You got a bucket of something awful that'll fall on top of me?"

"I don't blame you for being suspicious. I'd be suspicious too." I twisted the heel of my shoe back and forth on the rug. "You just seem a little down."

"Momma get you a rock tumbler already?"

With that, I burst out laughing, and Ivylee glared at me like she was watching me turn funny myself. "No. I'm not sure tumbling rocks could help me. Who knows? Maybe I'm beyond help." I tried to laugh, but when I glanced toward Ivylee to join in, a look of fear had spread itself all across her face. It had never occurred to me before that Ivylee needed me also, beyond running the farm. I was so taken aback by this thought that I didn't even know how I felt about it. "I'm just kidding," I shrugged, feeling as though I was stumbling over my own words. "Look, Momma made some lemonade earlier. I think I'm gonna go have a glass. Would you like one?"

Ivylee shook her head.

With my hand on the doorknob, I added, "If you decide

you want me to help you move your desk, just let me know."

"The sunlight gives me a headache."

"Really? I didn't know that. We could get a shade at the hardware store to filter some of it out."

Ivylee nodded. "Or maybe I could make one?"

"That would work. You'd need some bigger paper though. Maybe Jess over at the Jitney Jungle would let you have some of his butcher paper. It's white, and it might work."

Still cautious, she said, "And I could decorate it maybe with some paper doilies."

"That's a good idea." We stared at one another like we might have just met. "Well, I think I'll go have some lemonade."

Before I pulled the door to behind me, I heard, "Pour me one too. I'll come in a little bit."

Chapter 10

Runaway

From time-to-time, when the pressure of it all got to me so that I felt my only option was death, either theirs or mine, I would run away. Usually, I didn't run far, just far enough to appease myself or make myself think I had some control over my life. Most often I would end up at the old mill over near the railroad tracks, where I sat and listened and watched water as it poured over the dam. Occasionally, I considered joining the water, but figured my body would develop some new buoyancy it never had before and float forever. Or, should I drown, my lifeless body would anchor itself to a rotting, dead sea turtle that had somehow traveled great distances in search of a lost love or life and maneuvered its way into the Flint River where it found itself bogged down in the mire and debris by fishing line so strong that it could have certainly captured and contained the whale that swallowed Jonah. Either that or I would find myself trapped beneath the murky waters forever anchored to Miz Potter's holey coffin.

The two times I ran away, Momma called Sheriff Dorsey to find and pick me up. Next to Momma, Sheriff Dorsey was the truest kind person I had ever known, probably far too kind to be a sheriff; and he always knew where to find me—the same place we had played and swam as kids. J.D. would pick up a loaf of bread, bologna, and a couple of tomatoes for bologna sandwiches along with a couple bottles of Coke at the supermarket, drive over to the old mill and come and sit beside me while I threw rocks into the river. If it didn't look like I had gotten my fill of hearing rocks plunk into the water, J.D. would gather up handfuls of rocks for me. He knew why I was there, and we didn't need to talk about it.

Some people marry their best friend; I wasn't that smart. I had wanted to be a forest ranger, to live in either the north Georgia or north Alabama mountains. J.D. wanted to stay closer to home, to live on and farm his grandfather's land. I loved the land, but I had had enough of farming. As a child I had gone to Desoto State Park near Mentone and Fort Payne, Alabama and had fallen in love with the rich, green beauty in those deep purple-blue mountains, and I wanted to live in the serenity of it. I planned to attend two years at a junior college then transfer to a school that offered a degree in forestry. Near the end of my sophomore year, the call came from Momma to come home. I left school and never went back.

J.D. handed me another handful of rocks and sat down beside me.

"Skipping any today or just tossing?"

"Just tossing. Like to watch them sink to the bottom."

"Sink to the bottom, huh? You can't see the bottom."

"That's right."

"And what would you do if one came back up?"

"No chance of that."

"You never know."

"You may never know, J.D., but I do."

"And what makes you the expert on sinking. You got a degree in that?"

"No, but I got lots of experience."

"Experience doesn't count for everything."

I looked at J.D. for the first time since he had sat down beside me. "And this comes from a man riding around with a washcloth bunny rabbit in the back window of his patrol car? Are those your credentials?"

A crooked smile that he half-heartedly tried to suppress crossed his face as he looked down at the rock he moved about with his fingers, and I could feel my heart sinking. To emphasize the official capacity of his profession J.D. sat up straight. "Hey, lay off the bunny rabbit."

"She call you?"

"Yep. Took me a while to understand what she was saying. Didn't make much sense at first."

"Has anything she's said ever made sense?"

"In her own way, she has." After a long pause, J.D. added, "She cried this time. She's scared, Sister, and who could blame her? It's a lot for one person to hold together. A lot for one person to handle."

"She doesn't handle it. I do."

J.D. looked across the river like he wished he could find an answer for me there.

"I knew I was everybody else in town's 'Sister.' When did I become yours?"

We both studied the water cascading over the dam.

The sound of J.D's voice softened. "The day you left." J.D. tossed a rock into the water as though to punctuate his response.

I swallowed hard as regrets surfaced. "Why did you

marry her?"

J.D. looked at me for a long time before he spoke. "Because I didn't want to be alone."

Neither of us said anything for a while, as the river became a scrapbook of memories.

"Any regrets?" I finally asked, but not really wanting an answer.

"Life comes with built-in regrets. There's no need to go looking for them."

"Got an answer for everything, don't you? Does that come from keeping the peace?" I threw three rocks into the water one after the other with all the force I could put behind them.

Grinning like the cat that got the goldfish, J.D. answered, "Yep. Comes with the uniform. I put this badge on, and wisdom just starts oozing out of me. Must have punctured myself once with it."

"You sure it's wisdom?"

"Always the tough smart aleck, aren't you?" J.D. motioned his head toward the river. "You trying to knock some fish unconscious?"

"What's it to you? You protector of the fish too?"

J.D. laughed and shook his head. "Gonna give me a little attitude, are you? I'm not the enemy, you know?"

"Yes, you are. Everybody's the enemy; everybody in this life is the enemy. Hell, life itself is the enemy."

J.D. didn't respond, but reached over and gently took my hand.

My eyes brimmed over, and again I tried to swallow those regrets. My voice was so soft I could barely hear it myself. "Don't think I can do it anymore," I whispered.

"Nobody would blame you. I don't know how you've stood it this long. And if I had any answers for you, I would have already shared them. The only answers are ones you don't want to hear."

J.D. was right, but I wasn't about to open that door.

"What got to you this time?"

"I don't want to talk about it, J.D." There was a long pause filled with lost promises.

"Did you love him?"

I was so stunned I may as well have been standing naked in front of J.D. "How the heck did you know about that? Momma? Ivylee?"

"His wife is not exactly the shy type. Actually, she wanted me to arrest you."

"Why didn't you?"

"Afraid you'd be a bad influence on the other prisoners." J.D. grinned and pushed me with his shoulder. "You didn't answer my question?"

"I was hoping you would have the good manners to let it go."

"Since when have we ever had manners with each other?"

Like Momma, J.D. waited for me to say the right thing. "I don't know if I loved him or not. I don't think so, although it would probably speak better of me if I did. I think he was just an escape or the dream of one. He was using me, and I was using him."

J.D. sighed, but said nothing, and I wondered if in some way he felt that I still belonged to him.

"Give me some of those rocks." He removed a couple of rocks from my hand and tossed them far out into the river.

Neither of us said anything for while. We just waited.

"Your momma said something about your being a rock tumbler?" Confused, J.D. lifted my hand filled with rocks and with his other hand, pointed toward the river. "Is that what you call this?"

"No, not hardly." I couldn't help but chuckle. "She's trying to 'find me a talent' and has decided that tumbling rocks might be it." I shook my head in disbelief. "Yeah, listening to rocks tumble in a metal bucket would surely solve my problems. Maybe they would drown out the sounds of the ones tumbling in my head."

J.D. squeezed my hand in his.

I swallowed hard, looked down to our hands and then back to the river. "So my new calling in life is to be a rock designer, if you need a title. Rocks will be the answer to all my problems, will fulfill me, give me purpose, warm me on cold, lonely nights. I don't know why it never occurred to me before. Maybe I'm one of Bunk's blind bunnies."

"It has to. . ."

"Please don't say that. I'm going to barf if you finish that sentence."

Shaking his head, J.D. looked at me. "Now that's a pleasant thought. I was going to say it has to be ninety degrees out here. Why don't we go for a swim?"

"Oh. I thought you were going to tell me it has to get better."

"I wouldn't tell you that, because I don't blow smoke, and besides, it'll probably never be any better. You'll just wither away, a bitter old broad." J.D. burst out laughing before he could add anything else.

"I don't like you."

"I know," he added with that crooked grin. When I did not respond, J. D. scooped up a handful of mud and smeared it across my cheek.

"That's not funny."

"Depends on your point of view. From where I'm sitting, it's pretty dang funny." J.D. smeared another handful of mud on the other cheek.

"Stop. I'm not in the mood."

"Sure you are. You just don't know it." This time, he stood up, grabbed up two cupped hands full of mud and threw it on me.

When I responded with a look of shocked indignation, J.D. collapsed into laughter and then tromped into the river and started slinging water at me. He looked so ridiculous standing there near the edge of the river, dripping wet in his sheriff's uniform that I couldn't help but laugh. I scooped up a couple handfuls of mud and muck myself and ran toward him, but before I reached him, J.D. grabbed me by my arms to keep me from tossing my mud balls at him. As we wrestled in the river, I managed to get at least a part of one handful of mud into his hair before he scooped me up into his arms with as much ease as scooping up the mud. "You know, you're kinda dirty. I think you need to rinse off."

"Don't you do it, J.D.!"

With no more effort than tossing a basketball, J.D. flung me up into the air, but caught me before I hit the water and took me under himself. We both came up laughing, and J.D. stood and helped me to my feet. I wanted to hang onto him for a while, but I think he knew it was too tempting a place for both of us.

"Remember when we baptized Ivylee?" J.D. reminded as he pulled me back toward the riverbank.

"What do you mean we? You baptized her, and I had to give her my desert for an entire week to keep her from telling Momma."

With that grin that was all too personal to me, J.D. helped me onto the riverbank. "Yeah, but it was worth it, wasn't it?"

I smiled and agreed of course, because it was. Of all the things J.D. and I had shared together, torturing Ivylee was one of the better ones. "I don't think I ever recall seeing

Ivylee so mad. I thought she was going to put a hex on the two of us right there in the river. She threatened me all the way home and said she was going to stand up in prayer meeting on Wednesday night and tell the entire town what we had done, because she wanted every one to know how evil and vile we were. The prayer meeting part didn't bother me too much, but I knew if Momma and Bunk found out, we would be in a whole mess of trouble. As it was, I had to coax and bribe her most of the way home just to get her to calm down. Thanks to you, for an entire month, I ended up having to watch cartoons every afternoon on television instead of 'American Bandstand.' You know, now that I think about it, J.D., you were an expensive friend. You don't know how many times I had to bribe that little twit to keep her quiet."

"Well, quality is costly, you know?" J.D. teased as he picked a piece of pine straw out of my hair.

Our eyes met briefly, and my heart hurt momentarily for what could have been. "Awfully sure of yourself."

"No, I don't have to be. I'm sure of you. I always have been."

"And what did that get either of us?"

"Don't," he whispered with a pained look. "Don't go there."

I tried to laugh, but I wasn't fooling J.D. or myself. "Must get old being right all the time?"

"No, not really." J.D. intentionally changed the tone. "It's rather enjoyable. How about a sandwich, river rat?"

"May as well. If that's all you got to offer," I tried to tease. J.D. shook his head, and I watched as he crossed the grounds to his patrol car, his wingtip shoes squeaking as water squished from them with each step. J.D. was the only person who had ever been able to take me from an unpleasant place within myself to another level, to another state of mind. I knew that he was the best person for me, if not the right person, and I also knew he would always be there. He had been and always would be that soft place for me to land. I knew it, and I counted on it, and I also knew that he was most likely a much better friend than a mate.

After we devoured our bologna and tomato sandwiches and Cokes and had dried off enough that our clothes weren't soppy, J.D. drove me home. He pulled his black and white patrol car into the driveway, put it in park and paused. There was nothing more to say.

J.D. lifted my hand, gently kissed it and whispered, "Good night, Weezie."

Chapter 11

Happy Birthday

One year in celebration of Bunk's birthday, Momma took Precious to town. She had made arrangements with Leon at the hardware store to stay open after hours for the party. Ivylee had made party hats and decorations. Momma had baked a coconut cake the night before and had me pick up vanilla ice cream, ginger ale and chips from the supermarket. Momma had already gotten Superman plates, cups and napkins. Only a handful of people would be invited to the party, as Momma did not want folks staring at Precious and making him feel uncomfortable. Besides our immediate family, Leon of course would be there and J.D. and Pastor Mike. Momma usually invited our neighbors, Ernest and Ernestine, but poor Ernest passed away last year in a tragic accident, and Ernestine still mourned and suffered her loss.

"Poor Ernestine is just beside herself with grief and needs time to recover, and I want this to be a happy time for Precious. So we'll party with her later."

Joy Hardware had been one of Bunk's favorite places, and he would spend hours enthralled with its contents. Momma used to say that had she and Bunk not inherited the chicken farm from Bunk's Uncle Cirrus, Bunk would have probably gone into the hardware business.

Ivylee and I arrived at six o'clock to decorate for the party. Momma would bring Precious at six-thirty, and the guests would arrive shortly thereafter. In the back of the store, Leon had a table set up with a wrapped present on top. Instead of ribbon, Leon had tied elastic straps around the box, and instead of a bow, he had secured a black, toilet tank ball to the package. It made a memorable gift.

Leon and Bunk were best friends, and on more than one occasion, I had seen tears in Leon's eyes when he visited with Precious. Although Bunk was a couple years older than Leon, they had hung out together growing up. When Leon's brother, Sonny, died in a swimming accident, Bunk stayed at Leon's side from the moment he heard until Leon's little brother owned his final resting place. Leon and Sonny had been swimming at Inman Lake. Both were good swimmers, but Sonny developed a leg cramp while swimming to the middle of the lake, and Leon could not get to him in time. Leon blamed himself and would not hear differently from anybody besides Bunk. Leon was a devoted friend to Bunk before Sonny's accident, but after, Bunk became his brother.

Leon lived with his memories, but the door never seemed to close on those memories, and he was known to tie one on now and again. Once several years ago, Leon had been drinking all day, and by nighttime, he was as pickled as a red pepper in hot sauce. After he closed the store that night, he turned out all the lights, got his rifle, laid down on the floor in the doorway at the front of the store and started shooting out tires of the cars as they went past. Sheriff Dorsey, J.D., said he didn't even try to talk to Leon. He came and got Bunk instead. J.D. later told me that Bunk walked right up to the front of the store and as casual as you please said, "Leon, I sure hope you not gonna shoot me because I'm planning on going fishing tomorrow, and I haven't even dug any worms for bait yet."

J.D. said Leon looked at Bunk through glazed eyes, stood up and staggered over to the trashcan where he tossed the rifle. Everybody knew, so nobody pressed charges. Leon replaced all the tires and gave all the drivers a new hammer. Bunk never said a word about it. The next day the two of them went fishing.

At least once a month, Leon came to the house to get Precious to take him fishing, but Leon doesn't call him Precious. To Leon, he will always be Bunk, and he will always be Leon's best friend, but in deference to Momma, Leon called Bunk "Partner."

Momma had bought Precious a new pair of overalls for his birthday and had embroidered "Birthday Boy" on the bib of them. When Ivylee placed the party hat on his head, Precious looked like an eccentric party farmer celebrating the first birthday of his new tractor.

Leon shook Precious' hand and took him by the arm. "Come on, Partner, got some new gadgets in that I think you'll enjoy." Leon led him around the store showing him different pieces of hardware, and Precious paid attention most of the time. He appeared to be particularly taken with an electric spray paint machine, and I overheard Leon promise, "Tell you what. Next day I'm off, I'll come out to your place, and we'll do some painting with this thing."

"Oh, Leon, I've got just the place y'all can paint." Momma poured ginger ale over the scoop of vanilla ice cream I had placed inside each cup.

Pastor Mike arrived carrying an open box of books with a big bow on the side, and J.D. followed him with a gift wrapped in brown shipping paper.

J.D. kissed Momma on the cheek when he placed his gift on the table. "And how is the most beautiful girl in Joy, Georgia today?"

Momma blushed and giggled. "J.D., if you and I weren't already married to other folk, I'd marry you for sure."

"Now don't go tempting me, Momma. You know I been stuck on you for a long time." J.D. grinned and nodded toward Ivylee while he placed his arm around my shoulder for a friendly hug.

"J.D., you know I don't like you, so ain't no need to be nodding at me."

"Ivylee, mind your manners," Momma scolded.

"Manners are not justified for some people, Momma."

"Good manners are always justified. Right, Pastor Mike? You got any words of inspiration you can say to our Ivylee about her ungracious behavior?"

Pastor Mike cleared his voice self-consciously. "Well, be about the same thing I say ever week in church. That being, if we can't do nothing else, we can live by the Golden Rule. And if I can just get some of those folk to do that, I figure I'm at least doing half a job, and I'm counting on the Lord to help me with the rest."

"Amen to that," J.D. agreed. "And it's okay, Momma. Ivylee's got every right to dislike me. I've never given her any reason to do otherwise." J.D. winked at Ivylee, who stuck her tongue out at him.

Ivylee probably had less feeling for J.D. than she did for me. Growing up, J.D. had picked on her like an older brother, but because he wasn't blood-related, to Ivylee's way of thinking, she was under no obligation to excuse him, and she didn't.

One of the worst pranks J.D. ever played on Ivylee was putting a garter snake in her lunch box. For some reason, maybe to stay warm in that metal box, the snake had crawled into the wax paper around her fried bologna sandwich, and when Ivylee went to bite into the sandwich, the garter snake bit her on the lip instead. It scared Ivylee so bad that she wet her pants right there in the lunchroom, and all the kids laughed at her. Ivylee left school and refused to come back for three days, and it took some serious coaxing on all our parts to get her to come back then. J.D. vowed that he had not meant for it to go that far and felt bad about what had happened, but the damage was done, and for Ivylee, it would never be undone, no matter what J.D. did to try to make it up to her. And that was the last practical joke J.D. ever played on Ivylee, but even that did not matter to her.

"You can kiss where the sun don't shine, J.D. Dorsey. Sheriff or not, I got no use for you. And it just goes to show, some people will vote for anything, even a scum bag like you."

"Ivylee," Momma warned.

While I did enjoy watching the two of them torture one another, this was going a little too far. "Ivylee, that's uncalled for, don't you think? How long are you going to carry a grudge?"

"I don't know. How long is he going to live?"

J.D. burst out laughing. "You know you love me, Ivylee. You're just trying to hide it."

"You been drinking on the job? And it wouldn't take much to hide anything from you, J.D."

"I think we should get on with the party," Momma intervened. "Leon, bring that birthday boy over here to open his presents."

112

Leon escorted Precious back to the party table, and Momma pulled a chair out for him. "Here, baby boy. Sit down here and get ready to party." Momma guided Precious into his chair and placed one of the presents in front of him.

"Those are from me," Pastor Mike offered. "Thought you might enjoy some books. There's a couple of picture books in there and one on birds and one on gardening. Now you let me know if y'all find out anything new on tending roses in that one. Mine haven't been doing too well recently."

"And how are all those azaleas doing that you planted last year, Mike? Your place must look mighty nice with that many azaleas." Leon picked up a cup of ginger ale float and sipped it.

"Well, let's just say that if I were their preacher, I would have lost my flock and be heavy into funerals. As a matter of fact, most of them are dead. I didn't know not to fertilize them too soon, and I'm afraid I burned every one of them with fertilizer. Couldn't believe it. Went out there the next day, and all I had was eighty-something dead sticks in the ground. They looked like shrubs you might expect to find around Hades. I always hope the good Lord will protect me from myself."

"Oh, that's a shame, Pastor," Momma sympathized. "Maybe you can use the sticks as kindling. And you know what they say? 'God takes care of fools and children.' Guess He must have been busy that day though, huh?"

"Momma," I screeched. "Pastor Mike, I don't think Momma realized what she was saying."

"Oh, that's okay. She's probably right, and I've never doubted it for a minute."

"You misunderstand me," Momma explained. "What I meant was that I say that about myself. That is, that 'God takes care of fools and children,' and I've always known which category I fell into." Momma handed another gift to Precious and proceeded to help him open it.

"Momma, I think it would be best if you let this subject drop."

"Which category do you think I fall into, Momma?" Ivylee asked with sincerity like it was some club, and she didn't want to be excluded.

"Ivylee, you're in a category all your own," I answered.

Ivylee smiled like I had told her I thought she was a princess, and J.D. winked at me.

Leon motioned to the gift that Momma was helping Precious open. "That one's from me, Partner. I went around the store and gathered up every kind of gadget I thought you might enjoy tinkering with. Couldn't make up my mind what to use as a bow until I remembered you playing a trick on Sonny one summer and putting a toilet ball on his fishing line instead of a bobber. Sonny was so tickled that he could barely tell Pa what you'd done." Leon paused as if to hold on to the memory. "Anyway, there's all kinds of nuts and bolts and screws in there and a new measuring tape and even one of those old folding wooden ones we used to play with when we were kids. And if you see anything else around here you like, you just let me know, and it's yours."

J.D. looked at me, and I looked away.

"That's so nice, Leon. Isn't that nice, Precious? Look at that big black ball. My, but you'll have a time with that. Would you like to let it float in the pond?"

Precious held the tank ball tightly to his chest as though it might get away from him if he didn't. Although he didn't say a word that night, I had a feeling that somewhere inside he knew.

"Oh, you can have a time with all these treasures, dear."

Momma smiled, acknowledging Leon's thoughtfulness. When I glanced in Leon's direction, his anxious fingers fiddled with the watch in the bib pocket of his overalls.

"And this one's from me, Bunk, I mean Precious." J.D. glanced at Momma apologetically.

"He don't even know who he's here for," Ivylee taunted. "I hope you don't have this much trouble identifying folks on your job, J.D. You probably make some criminal's day every day."

"Drop it, Ivylee," I cautioned.

"Well, if I did know what I was doing, then I'd for sure come and get you, Sweetie Pea," J.D. teased.

Ivylee stuck her tongue out at J.D. again. "Can we have some cake now, Momma?"

"Sure we can, Honey. Leon, you got any matches?"

Leon and J.D. both pulled a pack of matches from their pockets and lit the candles on the cake.

Momma pushed the cake in front of Precious, leaned down and kissed him on the cheek. "Think you can blow these out by yourself this time, baby?"

Precious looked to Momma and then at the cake like he was trying to remember what to do. When nothing happened, Leon swallowed hard and turned away.

"It's okay, Sweetie. Momma will help you."

Momma made a wish and blew out the candles on Precious' cake again that year, while the rest of us looked anywhere but at the two of them and each other.

"Momma made a good wish for you, baby."

"How about if I say a little birthday blessing?" Pastor Mike asked.

"That would be nice, Pastor. Say anything you like. We appreciate it all." Momma straightened Precious' party hat. "Don't we, birthday boy?"

"Heavenly Father, please bless our dear brother who

celebrates another birthday. Unlike the candles on his cake, let your light not extinguish in his life. Please guide him along his path, and if it be thy will, along a path back to us. Bless each and everyone here. Bless this food to the nourishment of our bodies, and our bodies into thy service. Amen."

A soft chorus of "amen" sounded around the room.

"Thank you, Pastor. That was lovely." Momma cut large slices of coconut cake for everyone while I placed potato chips on each person's Superman plate. "Here, Precious, baby, you get the first piece."

Precious looked at the piece of cake, picked it up and placed it on the table. Then he folded his plate and placed it inside his pocket.

"Momma, I believe you make the best coconut cake in these parts," Pastor Mike complimented when Momma handed him his plate.

"You don't have to save your plate, Precious. I've got another one for you to take home." Momma placed Precious' piece of cake on another Superman plate. "Superman was Bunk's. . ." The word froze on Momma's lips, and all of us froze in response. Momma had not referred to Precious as Bunk since moving him to the tool shed. It was as though that part of her life was on hold, frozen in another time, waiting on cue to be recalled. Bunk was Bunk, and Precious was Precious. One's presence was manifested in the form of his leg inside the house; the other existed outside. Clear lines as to where each could exist had been drawn, and they did not cross.

I stepped forward and slipped the cake knife from Momma's hand. "Let me help you with that cake."

Momma turned to me and faintly said, "Sister?"

"It's okay. I don't mind. Besides, you've been doing all the work, and you were up late last night baking this cake."

"That's right," J.D. chimed. "You always did do too much. I remember that cake you made for our graduation party. I don't think I've ever seen a cake that big, and it was devoured within minutes. You had decorated it with a big graduation hat made of sugar and hung a tassel on each corner of the tray, remember?"

Momma's eyes focused on J.D., as he gently brought her back to where we were.

"Yes, I remember. It was a yellow cake." "That's right, and I never confessed this before, but I ate three other people's pieces of cake that night."

Momma half-smiled. "J.D.," she whispered.

"Could I please have my piece of cake now, Momma?"

Startled somewhat by the needs of one of her children, Momma turned her attention to Ivylee. "Yes, dear. I'm sorry. Guess I got distracted."

As I handed Ivylee a piece of cake and cup of ginger ale float, she motioned toward J.D. with her head, "This could go on all day with him. As if anybody cares what he does."

"Ivylee, please try to be a little kinder?" Momma pleaded.

"What is wrong with you, Ivylee? Did you drink vinegar today or something?" In addition to the disdain Ivylee had for J.D., she also could not accept Precious into either her reality or her make-believe, and it seemed to throw her off kilter when she was forced to do so.

"Sometimes I think Ivylee forgets her manners," Momma explained. "Ivylee, do you need to go sit in time out? I'm sure Leon has a time out chair here if we need it."

"Momma, I am not a child."

"Then stop acting like one," I said.

Ivylee took her piece of cake and chips and wandered to the front of the store.

"What's eating her?" J.D. whispered to me.

"Who knows?" I answered. "And furthermore, who cares?"

"Sister," Momma warned.

After we served everyone cake and chips, I took my serving over to a counter that jutted out from the wall. On top of the counter sat an old-fashioned cash register that Leon had allowed us to play with when we were kids. J.D. joined me there while Momma, Leon and Pastor Mike sat with Precious.

"Something wrong?" J.D. asked.

"No more than usual," I replied.

"Seriously, what's up with Ivylee?"

"I have no idea, J.D."

J.D. looked at me like he questioned the truthfulness of my response. When it became obvious that he had no intention of letting it drop, I added, "I overheard her and Momma talking, and if I had to guess, I'd say it's the same thing that's wrong with the rest of us—reality. I guess some days even Ivylee cannot make Momma's make believe work."

"The two of you need to get away for awhile before you completely lose your minds."

"Well, obviously, it's too late for Ivylee. And tell me, how are we supposed to do that, J.D.? You sound about as out of touch as Momma."

"The three of us could watch them for a weekend." J.D. motioned to the group sitting around the birthday table.

"J.D., I know you mean well, and I appreciate it. But this can't happen for reasons I don't even want to think about, much less talk about. And besides, going away with Ivylee would be like going to the beach to get away from the sun."

"Well, the offer's there if you ever change your mind."

"I appreciate it, truly. So, what did you give Precious

this year since he never got to finish opening your present?"

With his smug, self-assured, sheriff look, J.D. answered, "Gave him a rabbit, one made out of a washcloth, but wearing sunglasses." After I glared at him with more aggravation than his response warranted, J.D. added, "A wireless alert system. Actually, it's more for you guys than for Bunk. I'm hoping it will help you keep better track of where he is."

"That's sweet, but I don't know that she would trust it enough to use it. Following and fretting over him is a big part of her day. You know we had that sheep dog for a while, and it was supposed to stay with him and steer him away from the road and toward the house, but she started fretting over the dog about as much as she frets over Precious. I looked out the window one day and spotted her sitting on the front steps with Precious and the dog, both wearing bandanas, and sitting at her feet like she was the head mistress on a school field trip. And all the while she's talking to the two of them, she's breaking up a cheese biscuit that she took turns sharing between the two. It frustrated me so bad, I gave the dog to Shep Beasley that day to use on his farm. She wasn't none too happy with me about it, but I figured one more responsibility around there was one more than we needed.

"Anyway, it was good of you to do that, and we can certainly try using it, but I'd still hang on to my receipt if I were you."

J.D. shoved his last bite of cake into his mouth. "Good cake. Your momma makes the best cake in these parts."

"And thanks, J.D. For before."

J.D. nodded with a mouth full of cake. "Okay, Momma, do I get seconds tonight or are you putting me on a diet?"

"I know a growing boy needs to eat, J.D."

"Afraid the only place J.D. is going to grow at his age is out, not up," Leon teased.

"And we know he's never going to grow up," I added.

"Where's Ivylee's tongue?" J.D. asked as he pretended to look around.

While Momma was cutting second helpings for everybody to take home, I slipped quietly to the front of the store where Ivylee sat staring absent-mindedly at the street. For what seemed like forever, an awkwardness had loomed between us like thick smoke. I think we were both bitter for sometimes-the-same and sometimes-different reasons. Neither of our lives had taken us to where we thought we would be, and I think I resented her weakness, and she resented my strength. "Was good cake, wasn't it?"

Without looking up, she answered, "Yeah, but Momma's cakes are always good."

I motioned to the street. "You remember when we were in that parade? What was the parade for? It wasn't one of the holiday parades."

"The School Pride Parade."

"Oh, yeah. Everybody in school had to participate, and Mrs. Mendelson decided that all the Home Ec classes would wear something they had made."

Staring at the street like she could see the parade, Ivylee said, "And I wore that navy blue jumper that I had embroidered with some tulips."

"That's right. You had red, yellow and purple tulips embroidered across the front." Ivylee looked at me like she couldn't recall who I was. "And I wore that green skirt and top."

"You hated Home Ec, and Momma was always saying 'I don't know how we are going to get Sister through this class.'"

"And she was on the money with that." The atmosphere

120

was intense from the awkwardness between us. "I would have failed that semester if you had not snuck my sewing assignment out of the Home Ec lab and brought it home for you and Momma to finish, so I would have something to wear in the parade the next day."

"Momma had to take the skirt completely apart."

"And while Momma took the skirt apart and put it back together the right way, you basted the interfacing around the neck of the top and sewed the button holes."

"Momma said if you had been blind, she didn't think you could have made a bigger mess of that skirt and that she didn't know how anybody would be able to wear what you'd put together." Ivylee chuckled. "I know I would not have wanted to wear it."

"And I didn't know how I was going to get out of being in that parade. Mrs. Mendelson said that if we weren't there, we'd better be in the hospital somewhere," I added as I laughed. "I was trying to figure out if there was anybody in the county who would be willing to give me a disease." I moved closer to the window, next to the neon sign that advertised Leon's store. "I couldn't sew. Just didn't interest me. Of course, not much about Home Ec ever did."

"I loved Home Ec."

"Well, you were good at it."

Ivylee tilted her head as if she were waiting for something sarcastic to follow.

"Anyway, I don't think I ever thanked you for doing that."

Startled, Ivylee looked at me like a puppy upon realizing grasshoppers jump. "You've been acting so strange recently. Are you coming down with something?"

I shook my head. "I can see why you might think that." I cleared my throat in an effort to dislodge any sentimental trappings lurking there. "Look, I know we don't get along.

Most days we can barely tolerate each other, and some days, I don't think we even like each other. But I also know that you're my sister." Ivylee stared at me for such a long time that I began to feel uncomfortable. "Well, I'll go help Momma clean up."

As I was about to walk away, she said, "You're welcome."

"What?"

"You're welcome. For the Home Ec assignment."

I nodded and left. No need in taking this sister thing too far.

When I returned, Momma was gathering up the used cups and plates while the men were talking town business.

Precious pushed his chair back from the table. Unsteady on his feet when he first stood up, Precious ambled in our direction.

J.D. extended his hand to Precious. "Happy birthday, sir."

Precious looked at J.D.'s hand and moved away.

"He means no harm."

"I know that." J.D. motioned toward Ivylee. "She okay?"

"I think so. 'Bout as okay as she can be."

J.D. grinned and in his smug self-satisfied manner added, "I knew you'd do it."

"You did no such thing."

"You've always done what I've led you to do."

"You are so full of crap, J.D."

"It's true. Think about it."

"That so?" Nodding my head in mock agreement, I looked down at the little bit of ginger ale and foam still in my cup. "You're probably right." Smiling like a cat at an empty canary cage, I looked into J.D.'s eyes, reached up, pulled the pocket of his uniform shirt open, dumped the rest of the ginger ale float into it, and patted the pocket closed. "Think your wisdom may have sprung a leak."

With those masculine facial features highlighted by his self-assured air, he laughed in spite of his efforts not to. "You know what? If all these people weren't here, I'd spank your butt right now, which is exactly what you need."

"Yeah? You and what troop?"

Without so much as a beat, J.D. yelled, "Momma, your daughter's misbehaving."

"Which one, J.D.?"

"The sassy, smart-mouthed one."

"Now J.D., you know she's been like that all her life, and I haven't been able to do a thing with her." Momma studied the front of J.D.'s shirt. "How did you manage to spill your drink, J.D.?"

I threw my head back and howled. "He's clumsy, Momma. He always has been."

"Well, we're all clumsy at times. Why, I spilt a half-a-bottle of vanilla flavoring last night. We just have to be more careful, don't we, J.D.?"

When I howled again, Momma looked at me as though I had taken leave of my senses. "Did we step in it, J.D.?" I teased. Enjoying the meanness of the moment, I danced and sang, "'Great green gobs of greasy, grimy gopher guts.'" J.D. laughed and joined in on the second line. "'Medicated monkey's feet, Little bitty birdie's feet; Great green gobs of greasy, grimy gopher guts, and I forgot my spoon.'"

As we both paused to see which of us would add the last line, to our surprise, Ivylee finished it. "'But I got my straw. Slurp.'"

J.D. and I swapped looks of pleased amazement. For the first time in almost twenty years, Ivylee allowed J.D. to co-exist in something less than disdain, and we both knew to leave it where it lay.

With one hand on her hip and the other one across her heart, Momma chided, "Must you children sing that nasty song? It's not fit for civilized people and certainly not appropriate for a party. Pastor Mike, would you please speak to them?"

Pastor Mike stood before us contemplating the children, all of whom were adults, one of whom was the sheriff, and although he tried to suppress his smirk, the best he seemed able to offer was, "Now children, there's an appropriate place for everything, and if one of you finds where it is, I wish you'd tell me." Then he led us in another round of the song.

Momma threw up her hands and half-heartedly admonished, "Mike."

Leon laughed and added, "Don't know about you, Momma, but I think it's a lost cause."

While Momma continued to gather the remaining party supplies, Precious wandered around the store as though in search of something. Behind the counter with the old-fashioned cash register, he stopped and studied a faded photograph pinned to the wall.

Leon came and stood behind him. "It's the three of us—you and me and Sonny. Do you remember Sonny? We'd gone fishing down at Inman's Lake. We didn't catch a thing, but we had the time of our lives. When we got back, Pa teased us about it. 'Lemme get a picture of all them fish, boys.' And there we were with empty poles and empty buckets. You told Pa we'd gone snipe huntin' for fish, and Pa howled at that one. Sonny used to say they wouldn't nobody funnier than Bunk. All you had to do was look at him sideways, and he'd burst out laughing." Leon's voice softened to a whisper. "He was a good boy."

Precious said nothing, but continued to stare at the

photograph. Leon reached up and removed the photograph from the wall and placed it inside the bib pocket of Precious' overalls. "It's yours, Partner. Anything I got is yours."

Neither of us said anything for a while. Momma awkwardly covered the rest of the cake with the lid to the Tupperware cake plate, picked up the extinguished candles, and placed them in the paper bag.

As far as birthdays went, it had been both sweet and bittersweet, but regardless, it had been another one.

Chapter 12

Somebody's At The Door

As I sat in the living room stringing green beans for lunch, I heard Momma knocking on the board that encased the doorknob in the tree stump.

"Anybody there?"

Like a circus pony trained to perform, Momma appeared to wait for her cue, and when no answer came, on cue, she turned and entered the living room.

"'Behold I stand at the door and knock,. . .'" Momma recited as she stepped inside the room. Confused, she stopped, looked lost, and crossed the room to the sofa where she removed her Bible from inside the coffin and read, "'. . .if any man hear my voice, and open the door, I will come in to him, and will sup with him, and he with me.'" Momma looked up from her Bible as though to contemplate this passage just as a knock sounded on the screen door. Pale as a white petunia, Momma looked like she had seen every ghost in the graveyard come to call on her at one time. "He's here!"

I placed the pan of green beans aside to answer the door. With a hint of frantic in her voice, Momma whispered, "I don't think you should answer it."

"Why?"

Momma pulled her Bible to her chest as though to protect her heart and whispered, "I'm not ready."

"Ready for what?"

"I don't know what to serve."

"Who says you have to serve anything? Momma, you're starting to act more like Ivylee every day. That is not a good thing. Ivylee lives in la-la land. Now get hold of yourself."

"Here He is to 'sup,' and I don't know what to serve."

With frustration spewing forth like steam from "Old Faithful," I crossed the room to the screen door. A tall, lanky, sort of dopey-looking young man in an olive-green uniform stepped inside our living room like he was stepping over a mud puddle.

"Howdy, Ma'am. I'd like to introduce myself."

"There's no need. We know who you are."

"You do? What are you? One of them psychics?"

Fascinated, Momma appeared to have recovered from her previous state of panic. "We been waiting for you. I mean, I been waiting for you." Momma stood and snapped to attention like an "onward Christian soldier" about to be sent into religious warfare. "Brace yourself, Sister. My time has come."

"That's mighty nice you been waiting for me. How long you been waiting?"

"A long time, haven't we, Sister?"

"Since this morning," I replied. When conversations with Momma involved a third person, I had long ago concluded that the best approach was to try to ignore her, as it sometimes reduced the confusion.

Like a child who had solved a puzzle, Momma hurriedly removed the rock from the coffin and replaced it with her Bible. "'The Lord is my rock. . . The God of my rock; in him will I trust.'"

Looking through the screen door in the direction of his truck, I asked, "You our new chicken doctor?"

"Here he is to 'sup,' and all we got is beans and bread."

"We don't have to feed him, Momma. We didn't feed the last one."

"The last one didn't matter."

"Maybe not to you," I reminded.

Momma held the rock in her open hand like it was a peace offering. "Did you send us this rock?"

"No, Ma'am," the young man answered as he studied the rock. "Don't recall sending any rocks recently."

Momma stood in front of the stranger in the olive-green uniform and sized him up as though to evaluate him for a promotion. "You don't look at all like I expected. And you wear uniforms? Will I have to wear one too? I prefer blue myself. Don't care for army green at all. Never have. Makes me look peaked. I sorta thought you'd be wearing white?"

"What are you talking about, Momma?"

"They make the women folk wear green too, Ma'am."

"Well, I don't hold with breaking the rules, especially on the first day. Where is your crown?"

"Since when do you need a crown to cut open a chicken?"

"Oh, I ain't no chicken doctor, Ma'am."

"I knew it!" Momma chirped with delight as she ran to the screen door and looked out. "Aren't you supposed to have a band with you? Or do you do this part alone?"

"You play in a band?" I inquired with more surprise in

my voice than I could hide.

"Wouldn't exactly call it a band. Got a whistle out in my truck. Use it to call my dog."

Amazed, Momma echoed, "Dog. They allow dogs? Don't recall reading anything about dogs. Lambs, lotsa little lambs, but no dogs."

"Oh, they wrote you about me?" he asked, obviously pleased.

Momma idled up next to the stranger, leaned her head toward him and whispered, "I know this is kinda personal, but could I see your wounds? Just the ones on your hands will be fine. Musta hurt awful bad. Paper cut just about does me in."

"You been in the pickled eggs again, Momma? You know they make you light-headed."

"Ma'am, 'bout the only wound I got is some blisters from shoveling dirt."

"Exactly who do you think this is, Momma?"

"You did come here to save me, didn't you," Momma pleaded.

"Oh, yes, Ma'am. I'm hoping I can save you lots, I surely am."

Fearful that Momma had ordered some outlandish apparatus Ivylee had convinced her to buy, I quickly intercepted, "We ain't looking to buy."

"And I ain't looking to sell, Ma'am. I'm looking to serve. That's my job. That and looking for signs. Been looking for signs all my life. My poppa always said we living in the days of 'Revelations' and told me I needed to be looking for signs. And that's why I got me this here job."

"'Revelations,'" Momma repeated. "When do you start?"

"Just as soon as I can get a proper reading on your meter, Ma'am."

"You gotta put a meter on me?"

I quickly stepped in front of Momma in the improbable event Momma's question carried any validity. "You ain't messing with my Momma. I don't care what she's ordered from you."

"But that's the only way I can save her."

Momma peeked her head around me like a child playing peek-a-boo. "What will my meter measure? The depth of my soul? What if it ain't deep enough?"

"Your soul? Oh, no, Ma'am. Leastways, I don't think it does, but I'll pray for it, if'en you want me to."

Both puzzled and pleased, Momma toddled across the room to the sofa, removed her Bible from the coffin and proceeded to scan the "Concordance."

It had not taken long to recognize that the person in our living room was not necessarily blessed with brilliance. "Are you one of them evangelists? No wonder you're acting so strange."

"Oh, no, Ma'am. The Lord never blessed me in that way."

"You wouldn't be the first one of them he didn't bless. And it appears that all that got blessed with some of them is their pockets."

A smile of recognition that could have served as a beacon in a lighthouse lit up the young man's face. "Ain't that the gospel truth. Why, this one place I worshipped, I had to buy a pew so's I'd have a place to sit. They let me put it in memory of somebody though, so I put it in memory of my Uncle Oochie. He was a moon shiner. Brought happiness to lotsa folks, so I figured he needed remembering as much as anybody."

"My Bible don't say nothing about meters," Momma confirmed.

"No, Ma'am. Don't reckon it does, but I expect reading

meters for power is right respectable, don't you?"

"You read meters for power! What kinda power? The Lord's power? Read the Bible for power myself. Powers me in all kinds of ways, except I don't reckon I understand a lot of it." Momma stopped and studied the stranger like he might be turning into a toad. "You know, you sound awful peculiar for a Savior. You are my Savior come to fetch me home, aren't you?"

Shock crossed the young man's face like lightning had passed through him. With long, lanky strides, the stranger paced back and forth while flailing his arms up and down as though he were a puppet with his arm strings being pulled. In a voice that left no doubt, he announced, "Oh, no Ma'am! No, sir-ree, Ma'am!!!"

"Then who are you?"

The stranger stopped, regained his composure, stood at attention and smiled like he was about to declare us winners in the game of life. "I'm your new meter reader, Ma'am."

"New meter reader! Did I have an old one?"

"Yes, Ma'am, but he said he had to go find himself."

"He must be some more lost soul."

"Yes, Ma'am, said he lost himself on one of those trips he was always taking."

Just when I thought that nothing Momma said had the ability to surprise me anymore, she piped up with, "Well, if you're not my Savior, did you come here to marry one of my girls? Ivylee's been waiting."

"Came here to read your meter, Ma'am."

"You can thank your lucky stars for that, Mister. I wouldn't wish Ivylee on Satan himself." Since the conversation appeared to be taking a turn toward the even-more-bizarre, I returned to the chair and to stringing beans.

"Don't believe in luck. Believe in lot, lot in life. That's

what I believe."

"Not already married, are you?" Momma toddled back to the sofa where she patted the cushion next to her as an invitation for the young man to join her.

"No, Ma'am. Was about to be divorced. My wife left me, up and left one day, ran off with an auctioneer. Going to be on the selling circuit, she was."

"Why'd she leave? You an ax-murderer?"

"Oh, no, Ma'am. Haven't operated an ax in years. Last time I did, the head came off, flew across the yard, and planted itself in a dogwood tree. Scared the ever-living daylight out of me. Thought I'd be sentenced to purgatory for sure."

"Bet it's a sign."

"My wife said it was a sign all right, a sign that I was a dim-witted, do-gooder whose fairy tale Bible stories counted for nothing. My wife wouldn't a believer, 'cept in herself. She believed herself to be 'better than the average bear,' as they say, and she could sure be a bear all right. Sometimes it gave me pause to wonder why I ever married her. Yeah, my Barbara left me, left me 'cause I'm lazy and good-for-nothing."

"You and Ivylee got a lot in common then." As I listened to this conversation, I was reminded of Abbot and Costello's "Who's on First," and I was equally amused.

"You got any kids," Momma pried.

"No, Ma'am. My wife said she had all she could handle cursing me."

"That so? My, she musta been a handful."

"Actually, more of a bucket, Ma'am."

"When did your wife leave you?"

"Friday, a week ago. Didn't get far though."

"How come? You didn't shoot her, did you?"

"Oh, no, Ma'am. I leave that kinda thing to God. As

best we can tell, my Barbara was sitting up in a tree, watching for her new man when one of these tree-trimming trucks comes along and trims her limb right out from under her and drops her into this limb-chomper. Chewed her up like sausage, it did."

"Oh, how dreadful," Momma grimaced.

"Ain't it though? Wouldn't wished it on a rattlesnake, no matter how mean she was. Guess they couldn't hear her yelling because about that time, the Blue Angels were flying over in them big ole jets for some show they were putting on over in Atlanta. So my Barbara got eaten by a big, tree-chomping truck that was drowned out by the sound of Blue Angels. Keep thinking there must be a sign in that, but ain't rightly figured it out yet."

This story was so outlandish that I had stopped stringing beans to listen. "Are you making this up?"

"Oh, no, Ma'am. Ain't that talented."

"My, my. Did you have a big funeral for her?"

"Nope. Can't figure out where to put her. Buried her in the pasture underneath the persimmon tree, but the pigs dug her up. So I got her on ice over at the mortuary. Don't take up much room now though."

At this point, I realized that "Who" wasn't on first, second or third, and I wasn't sure this "Who" was even in the game.

"That so?" Momma questioned. "Well, I'm looking forward to your meeting my Ivylee. You'll take to her right off. She's alive, you know."

"That's good."

"She's real pretty and got a real talent too."

As I surely didn't want my conscience to worry me later in the unlikely event this stranger took Momma seriously, I felt obliged to make a contribution since the conversation involved Ivylee. "Got a talent for worrying.

Could worry the wings off a fruit fly."

"Pay no mind to Sister. She's feeling a mite ornery because the chicken doctor's wife was gonna shoot her, but I fixed it for her. Of course, she don't have no chicken doctor, but she's alive."

"That's questionable."

"Now don't fret, Sister. I'm gonna find one for you too. Made up my mind this morning, but in the meantime, you can tumble some rocks."

Momma's conversations often came in bits and pieces, and sometimes it would take weeks to put all the pieces together. In both words and actions, Momma was definitely mysterious, but it was most often by accident.

Momma placed her hand on the young man's arm. "What'd you say your name was?"

"Hornblower, Ma'am. Gabriel Godfrey Hornblower."

For a moment, Momma looked like she'd been stung by a bee. "We'll just call you Meter Reader."

"And I best be getting about it, Ma'am." The young man stood up to leave.

"That's right. Now you go on and find your power. And we'll wait for you. We good at waiting, especially Ivylee. She's been waiting on Mr. Robinson for more than nine years now, and she won't up and leave you for no auctioneer either. She don't care for them fast-talking types."

"That's mighty important, Ma'am. Leaves a fella feeling mighty low when his one and only up and leaves. My wife said I was so slow, I wouldn't even know she was gone, but I did. When I went to put my boots on and nobody said, 'Only a fool would lace his boots like that,' I knew she was gone."

"Ivylee ain't that particular."

"That's right," I added. "Ivylee won't care if you lace

them through your pants. As a matter of fact, you'll be lucky to get your pants on with Ivylee."

"Your Ivylee, she's starting to sound better and better." Meter Reader grinned like he had discovered his rainbow or at least the pot at the end of it, which, to my way of thinking, would be empty if it happened to involve Ivylee.

"Now you go read your meters, and if you read anything good out there, you come tell me. I'm looking for power too, you know. That's why I read my Bible. It powers me in all kinds of ways, except I don't rightly know what to do with it."

"Wherever you get your power, Ma'am. Well, I best go read them meters. Can be real inspiring sometimes." Meter Reader walked onto the porch with Momma following behind and me following Momma with the pan of beans and a paper bag with the ends and strings of the beans. At the tree stump, Meter Reader stopped to examine the doorknob. "That's a mighty interesting doorknob, Ma'am. Where's it go?"

"Don't rightly know. Can't find the key. Knock every day, but nobody answers."

"That so," Meter Reader considered. "Might be the doorway to heaven. Where'd you get it?"

"Reckon somebody left it here, but nobody's claimed it yet. Sister thinks a tornado dropped it." Momma pointed to the sign and then to the gravestone. "Left that sign and that gravestone too, but don't know who's in the grave. Stone says it's an atheist."

"Nooo."

Momma nodded her head in agreement like a young child telling on an aggravating big brother.

"Bet it's a sign for sure, Ma'am." Meter Reader leaned toward Momma as though to share his most secret secret. "You know that ax I told you about? Well, that wouldn't the whole story. Later that summer, a storm came up, and it was thundering and lightning like it was the end of time. Well, lightning struck that ax head stuck in the dogwood tree and split that tree right down the middle all the way to the roots. Scared me so bad I spent the rest of the night underneath my bed praying into the floor. Next morning when I got up my courage to crawl out from underneath my bed and go look at that tree, well, that ax head wouldn't nowhere to be found. Was gone. I figure God came and took that ax head, and I ain't touched an ax since. And you know what?"

"What," Momma, who was completely enthralled, whispered. Wide-eyed and open-mouthed, her face looked like that of a young scout sitting around a campfire, mesmerized by stories of the boogey man.

"Well, the next spring when all the stuff starts sprouting and blooming, that dogwood tree bloomed. And you know what?"

Momma shook her head only slightly as if any movement might interrupt the safety of the story and bring the boogey man to life.

"It became two. Where there was one, now there are two! I think on that every day. Even built me platform in front of the dogwood tree and put a chair on it so's I can sit and think on it. Two," Meter Reader echoed as he held up two fingers as proof.

Momma swallowed hard like she was trying to charge the engine of her voice box. "And what'd you think?"

"I think it's a sign. Just like I think your doorknob is a sign."

Momma had finally found a kindred spirit. With her hands together in front of her, Momma looked like she was about to receive communion. "What'd you think it's a sign of?"

"Ain't figured that part out yet, but I'm a-working on it.

And I tell you what, Ma'am, if I happen across the key to that door while I'm looking for your meter, I'll stop and bring it to you, I surely will."

Momma's face lit up like a child's on Christmas morning. "Why, ain't you a fine feller. And I tell you what, if you happen across any haunts out there looking for a home, would you tell them we think it might be in our front yard? Except I don't want no atheist living in my yard, so they gonna have to move. I don't hold with being unfair to anybody, but I have my own beliefs, and this ain't one of them. Plain don't want 'em nowhere around. Would be a-feared God might get us mixed up in the confusion."

"I understand what you're saying, Ma'am." Meter Reader looked at the gravestone, nodded his head in disbelief and with a tone of sympathetic despair concluded, "Some poor soul's been displaced by life."

I stood at the screen door with the pan of string beans in my arms and watched as the two religious philosophers exchanged nods of complete accord.

"Ma'am, maybe the one that brought you that doorknob brought you this rock. Maybe the rock is the key."

Momma removed the rock from her apron pocket. "You think so? But I don't think it will fit in the lock." Like a wrapped birthday present, Momma shook the rock next to her ear as if doing so would reveal its contents.

Inspired, Meter Reader snapped to attention. "'. . .who *is* the rock save our God?' Psalms 18:31. *Maybe* somebody brought you a little piece of God."

When Meter Reader said this, Momma was so startled that her eyes looked like those of a baby bird, and she studied the rock as if afraid of it. "Oh, my. What do you think I'm supposed to do with it?"

"Don't rightly have the answer to that, Ma'am—

"I best put it up some place safe and save it then."

"But I'll think on it while I'm looking for your meter."

"You do that, Son. And you be sure to come tell me what you find out there."

"Yes, Ma'am. I will. I surely will. You got my word."

Momma watched as Meter Reader bounced down the front steps like a puppy gone out to play. As he searched the yard for our meter, Momma looked on in curious anticipation. "Kinda like looking for Easter eggs, isn't it?" Momma turned toward me, studied the pan of green beans, and added as casually as crossing a footbridge on a spring day, "Sister, if you don't get them beans on, we ain't gonna have nothing to feed Meter Reader on his wedding day."

"Feeding Meter Reader ain't exactly weighing heavy on my mind right now, Momma."

"Now don't pout. I'm gonna find one for you too, but right now I gotta go wake Ivylee and tell her she don't have to wait for Mr. Robinson no more, although he was kinda like a son to me."

"Mr. Robinson is a delusion."

"Would you like to wait for Mr. Robinson, Sister?"

"No, thanks. I'd just as soon wait for the second coming."

"Would you," Momma turned toward me and smiled as sweet surprise filled her eyes. "And all this time, I suspicioned you might be faking it, Sister. Just does my heart good to hear that. Maybe we could marry you off to a minister."

"I'd rather marry an undertaker. Least you know where they gonna take you."

"Wonder if Mr. Robinson is a man of God."

"Mr. Robinson doesn't exist."

"Well how could he be a man of God if he doesn't exist?"

"Please try to make some sense, Momma. Life is

difficult here at best."

"Life is a storm, Sister, and sometimes you just gotta find your safe place."

"My place or my 'displace?'"

With a smile that suggested reward, Momma looked in Meter Reader's direction. "He does seem like a nice young man, doesn't he?" Pleased with herself, Momma turned and entered the house. "In the meantime, I've got to find some place to put this rock. Might be a piece of God."

Uncertain that I wanted to allow myself to consider that possibility, I followed Momma inside. Just as she stepped inside the screen door, she squealed with pride and scurried across the living room to the sofa, where she sat, opened the coffin and gently placed the rock back inside. "Just where I had it before. In a safe place."

As I made my way down the hall to the kitchen, I could hear Momma singing, "'Rock of Ages, cleft for me, Let me hide myself in Thee;. . .'"

Chapter 13

Can't You Get That?

Sometime later, I was cleaning up the kitchen after canning ten quarts of peaches when I heard another knock at the door. I assumed it was Meter Reader come to report back to Momma on his findings, and so I continued with my work since Momma was in the living room reading her Bible and could surely answer the door. A few minutes later, I heard yet another knock and someone call out.

When I entered the living room, I found Momma sitting in the center of the sofa, apparently mesmerized by the Bible passage she was reading. "'For we are but of yesterday, and know nothing, because our days upon earth are a shadow. . .'"

As I dried my hands on my apron, Momma sat as still as the coffin in front of her, and her eyes appeared to dart back and forth about the room in anticipated apprehension. "You could have answered it, Momma. I'm trying to get done with the peaches."

"No, I couldn't."

"Why not? Have you tied yourself to the sofa again? You are starting to act too strange for words, and if it doesn't stop, I'm going to stick you in one of them hospitals and let them give you some shock treatments."

Ignoring me, Momma repeated, "I know nothing, and my days are a shadow."

Spewing frustration, I may as well have been one of the Mason jars I had sterilized with steam. Nothing in the last nine years had prepared me for what was about to unfold. Bunk was at the door! Not as Bunk and not as Precious, but as Mr. Robinson. Dressed in his best overalls and with his hair combed and himself as clean as a newborn babe after its first bath, he stood before me with his hand extended and smiling like he might have swiped all the cookies in the cookie jar without getting caught. The day thus far had been such a fiasco that I felt myself to be sinking into an unexplainable nightmare that became more psychedelic with each passing hour, and I began to wonder if someone was slipping drugs into my drinks.

I stepped back to allow "Mr. Robinson" to come inside and heard myself murmur, "I don't believe this. And yet I don't know why I say that. At this point, I should believe anything."

Momma's eyes darted in my direction. "The someone at the door told me to tell you, Momma. . ." At that moment, whatever this Mr. Robinson had said to me evaporated from my mind. "What was it you told me to tell her?"

The voice attached to whomever was on the other side of the door repeated, "'. . .neither is there any rock like our God.'"

With a look of surprise, Momma slammed her Bible

closed with the slap of her hands, opened the coffin, and removed the rock we had received earlier. "Oh, my, it's him."

When I saw Momma's response, I tried to reassure her. "It's Precious, Momma."

"Precious," she asked as she tried to put whatever picture floated through her head into some sort of frame.

From the other side of the door, came the question, "If I can't come in as Precious, can I come in as Mr. Robinson?"

"Does he look like Mr. Robinson?"

"Momma, Mr. Robinson doesn't exist. He could look like anybody."

"I don't think Mr. Robinson is that common, Sister."

"No, and I don't think this is Oz either, but apparently the last tornado has taken us some place else on the planet."

"Why would he say he's Mr. Robinson if he's not?"

"I don't know. I only maintain the funny farm, not its inmates."

At that moment, Bunk/Precious/Mr. Robinson, any and all of the aforementioned, resolutely entered our living room.

What had impressed me most about my daddy, when he was my daddy, was his warmth and the ease with which he drifted through life. My memories of him were soft and quiet like the man. He possessed an inner sweetness and naivety that suggested he was not adequately equipped to preside in this world. Up until the time of his accident, it was Momma who seemed to be the protector in our family. The man who was entering our living room was someone else, someone I had never encountered.

With a warm, almost magnetic grin, Mr. Robinson announced, "I've been wrestling with the devil."

Momma looked questioningly at me. "I've been in the kitchen, Momma."

This was a new game, and I was curious as to how Momma was going to weave it into our present, although questionable, reality.

"Well, Ivylee's the one that's been waiting for him, so you best go tell her, Sister."

Feeling as though Momma had thrown me a surprise birthday party complete with all my favorite movie idols, I scurried to the hall door and yelled with such pleasure in my voice that I surprised even myself, "Ivylee? Your prayers have been answered. Your Mr. Robinson is finally here! Come to take you away from all this drudgery and back to your beautiful home in Miami." As I waited to watch my surprise birthday present open itself, I muttered to myself, "Now this is going to be rich." Whatever had happened this day, prior to this moment, was about to be remunerated.

As Ivylee scrambled down the hall into our inner sanctum, she squealed like a baby pig about to be separated from its mother, "My Mr. Robinson is here? Has finally returned to take me away?"

With open arms, Mr. Robinson limped across the room. "My little Ivylee."

Ivylee stopped stone cold dead in her tracks. With a look of horror on her face that to me was priceless beyond measure, Ivylee yelled, "You are *not* my Mr. Robinson!"

Overcome with delight, and finally feeling rewarded for most of Ivylee's shenanigans, I asked with an overly appropriate amount of sincerity in my voice, "Aren't you happy to see him, Ivylee?"

"You stop that this instant! I know who this is."

"No, you don't, because you said he didn't exist."

"And you said Mr. Robinson didn't exist. So there."

Momma, who is always guided by good manners as well as the desire to keep her girls from bickering, instructed, "Invite the nice man to sit down, Ivylee."

"Why? Who's going to entertain him? I'm not. I'm getting married. You said so. Remember?"

"Mind your manners, Ivylee." Momma placed the rock inside her apron pocket and returned to the sofa.

Grinning with more than justified delight, I motioned Mr. Robinson inside.

"You'll have to excuse Ivylee. Sometimes she forgets she's not poor, white trash," I said as I pointed to the sofa.

"Oh, that's okay. I remember how my little Ivylee was. Always was one to say what's on her mind." Mr. Robinson slowly ambled across the room.

"Which was absolutely nothing, right? Oh, you must be Mr. Robinson. Only someone who knows Ivylee intimately would know that." I turned to Ivylee to give her my most ungenuine smile.

"He does not know me intimately. I have never been intimate with a fat man."

"Your graciousness is exceeded only by your good manners, Sister," Mr. Robinson complimented.

"Well, that's about all there is—grit and graciousness in the face of overwhelming odds, and the odds don't get anymore overwhelming than they are around here."

Momma looked down at the Bible in her lap like she was confused as to how it got there and then remembered. "Welcome to 'Robin's Rest.' Are you a shadow, Mr. Robinson?"

"Why, no, I don't think so."

"This man is not Mr. Robinson," Ivylee demanded.

Momma closed her Bible and placed it inside the coffin. "Would you care for something to drink, Mr. Robinson? It's about time for our afternoon snack."

"Uh, yes, I believe I would."

"Everything's all laid out, Sister. Just bring an extra glass."

144

I was about to leave the living room when Ivylee whimpered, "Mr. Robinson would be most upset to know a short, fat, bald man was going around impersonating him. I know he would, even though he is kind. And you could be the devil for all we know, Strange Man."

"Are you the devil, Mr. Robinson?" Momma asked as she carefully considered this possibility.

"Often had a devil of a time, but no, don't believe I'm the devil."

When I returned with the tray containing a pitcher of lemonade, four glasses and a saucer of saltine crackers, the three of them sat staring awkwardly at each other. I held the tray in front of Momma as she poured each person a glass of lemonade and handed it to them. With the saucer in her hand, she asked, "Won't you have some saltines, Mr. Robinson? I just love soda crackers with my lemonade. I consider it one of our finer delicacies."

"Why, thank you. I believe I will partake, dear lady."

Momma's face lit up like an angel's atop a Christmas tree. "Isn't he just precious, girls?"

I placed the tray on the sideboard and removed my own glass of lemonade. Ivylee, who appeared to be reaching her limit of maximum aggravation, warned, "And that's exactly who he is, so please stop referring to him as Mr. Robinson."

I, on the other hand, had not reached my maximum in total pleasure over this situation. "Would you prefer we call him Muffin Man?"

"How dare you discuss my muffins in front of a stranger."

"I didn't know you could cook, Ivylee," Momma said.

With the innocence of a lamb following behind a ewe, Mr. Robinson added, "I just love muffins."

Outraged and flustered like a bantam rooster, cocked

and ready to fight, Ivylee screeched, "Why, you filthy little fat man! You make one move toward my muffins, and you'll be wearing a pair of hooks for the rest of your life. Do you hear?"

Taken a-back by Ivylee's comments and reaction, Mr. Robinson looked like he might have just discovered he had entered the ladies restroom by mistake. "Why, certainly. I would never touch your muffins without your permission."

"And you never will touch them either. Who told you about my muffins? Have you murdered my Mr. Robinson? Only death could get him to reveal the intimacies of our wonderful sex life in our beautiful home in Miami."

Momma, who was as equally confused as Mr. Robinson, questioned, "Sex?"

Mr. Robinson followed with, "Miami?"

Although I was enjoying this repartee more than I can say, I felt obliged to offer an explanation to Mr. Robinson. "It's make believe. Make believe is Momma and Ivylee's favorite pass-time. As a matter of fact, it's amazing how much time has passed. . ."

"I don't think we should be talking about sex at this time of day," Momma interrupted.

"Time passed," I repeated, "tending eighteen thousand mindless chickens that we nourish for nine weeks and then have slaughtered, only to do it all over again. It's like riding a bicycle with no brakes down a steep hill, only you can't stop, and you're not allowed to crash."

"But we've always been chicken farmers. That's what this place is, a chicken farm," Momma explained as if that fact had eluded me.

"And what would we do if we didn't have the farm? I can't work much, not since I got so sick that time," Ivylee added.

With a look of sympathy, Mr. Robinson turned to

Ivylee. "Yes, I remember."

Mr. Robinson's sympathy only inflamed Ivylee's fuel. "That's a lie. I'm not even sure you exist."

"Maybe you were too sick," Mr. Robinson offered.

"I'd have to have been dead."

"Maybe you were. Maybe we all are," I announced.

Confused beyond her capacity, the ninny asked, "Was I, Momma?"

"I don't think so. I think I would have known if you were dead."

"I'm not so sure." I replaced my empty glass on the tray and explained to Mr. Robinson, "Ivylee just sorta checked out on us for a while, and when she checked back in, her load had been lightened, so to speak."

"And what's that supposed to mean?"

"Oh, nothing, Ivylee. Except you have a lot in common with those chickens out there. I get that same blank look from them." Momma handed me the saucer containing the saltine crackers with the rock in the middle of them.

"Yes, Sister. I know all about those looks you get from the chickens," Ivylee taunted with a giggle.

"Ivylee," I warned with both a tone and a look that suggested certain death. "Eighteen thousand chickens and two cuckoo birds, 'this it is and nothing more.'"

Mr. Robinson seized the opportunity to rejoin the conversation. "'Quoth the Raven, 'Nevermore.' My favorite poem."

"You and Ivylee got a lot in common then. Ivylee writes pleasing poetry. As a matter of fact, it pleases her so much it's the only thing she can bring herself to do." I removed the rock from the saucer and laid it on top of the stove.

"I didn't know," Mr. Robinson responded with a note of surprise as he stood to replace his glass on the tray. "Ivylee, you never told me."

"And why should I? I'm not in the habit of sharing my privates with strangers."

"Ain't she genteel?" Mr. Robinson responded as he ambled toward the screen door.

"Only lack of work can describe how genteel she is," I answered.

"This is growing tiresome," Ivylee whined. "Can we please do the service so we can get it over with and go to bed? Oh, and I've got a new poem for you, Momma. It came to me last night when I was wishing upon a star."

Like a jack-in-the-box, Ivylee popped up and crossed the room to the old stove. From inside the oven, she removed a gourd dipper. As the rock did not appear to be an appropriate prop for this poem, Ivylee handed the rock to Mr. Robinson, who simply took it and said, "Why, thank you."

Ivylee stepped up onto the oven door and then to the top of the stove. Using a gourd dipper as a microphone, Ivylee declaimed, "'The Big Dipper' by Ivylee. 'Is the Big Dipper half-empty or half-full? Does it encase a drink for me? Or just drip darkness across the night? Purple darkness that drips out daylight.'" While she waited for Momma's adulation, Ivylee held up both arms as though finishing a performance as Shakespeare's Ophelia at The Royal Theatre.

Momma stood and applauded; Ivylee reveled; and although Mr. Robinson looked confused, he applauded also.

"That was lovely, dear. And speaking of star, would you please go get our little star out of the freezer? Ivylee is right. We need to get on with the service. It's past time, so let's get everything ready."

As Ivylee stepped down from the stove, Mr. Robinson extended his hand to assist her. "Excuse me. Did I miss something?"

"No," Ivylee answered. "It's in the freezer." Ivylee handed Mr. Robinson the gourd dipper and left the living room.

"Let's just put it in the ground," I pleaded.

"No, Sister. I told you. I flatly refuse."

"Well, I'm not going to participate."

"Oh, yes, you are. What would poor Bunk think if you didn't?"

"Frankly, I don't care. There's only so many times you can carry on over a chopped-off leg."

Momma grimaced before she replied. "Don't say chopped-off. Say amputated. Chopped-off sounds so harsh."

I shook my head in disbelief and turned to Mr. Robinson. "She keeps an amputated leg in the living room half the time, and she thinks saying 'chopped-off' is harsh."

From the barnyard, a rooster crowed three times. Appearing alarmed, Momma stood at attention and announced, "'. . .Watch ye therefore: for ye know not when the master of the house cometh, at even, or at midnight, or at the cock crowing, or. . .'" Momma paused to recall. ". . .or something."

Mr. Robinson looked on in awe and disbelief as Momma ran to the front porch to check the rooster clock that still sat among the roots of the tree stump. As he followed Momma onto the porch, she said, "You'll have to excuse us, uh. . ."

"Believe I'm Mr. Robinson."

"Oh, yes. Well, we have to get ready for the service. Maybe you could stay out here, and we'll wait for you some more."

Undaunted by all the confusion, Mr. Robinson followed Momma back inside. He looked baffled like he was trying to solve a puzzle. "The service?"

With this question, Momma's proof was validated. "See. What did I tell you, Sister? And that's why we have a memorial service."

"In memory of the dead, Momma. Not dead body parts. Just put the dang thing in the ground."

In spite of my pleas, Momma continued to prepare the living room for our next memorial service while Mr. Robinson watched. With his eyes following Momma around the room, he looked like a new player in a board game with confusing rules.

Chapter 14

Prepare To Be Serviced

Against my will, we prepared the living room for another memorial service for Bunk's leg, which enjoyed a fuller life in death than we did in life. Momma was beside herself with glee and anticipation as she scurried about the room making last minute preparations for the party wake. The only thing missing was cake and ice cream and goofy-looking paper hats. We had the piñata, no doubt the donkey one, as I impatiently waited to have the stuffing knocked out of me yet one more time.

"Mr. Robinson, could you help Sister move the coffin to the top of the sideboard? It gives Bunk's leg a better view."

"Oh? Why, yes." Mr. Robinson took hold of one end of the coffin while I took the other one. Together, we lifted and moved the coffee table/coffin to the linen-draped sideboard. "Be my pleasure," he added.

"Speak for yourself. I have yet to find anything

151

pleasurable about sitting through one of these, and once you've sat through a few thousand, I dare say you won't find any pleasure in them either."

"Sister, will you please stop being an old poop?" Just as soon as Momma finished chastising me, she turned to Mr. Robinson and added, "Sometimes Sister has a hard time seeing the sunny side of life."

"Momma, the sunny side of life could never include a coffin. Otherwise it would be the cloudy side of death. Just put the dang leg in the ground, and we can end this argument?"

"I cannot put it in the ground, Sister. It's all I have left of my poor Bunk."

Just at that moment, Ivylee danced into the room with the deceased piece wrapped in white paper. While Ivylee waited, Momma removed the middle sofa cushion and placed it behind the sofa. In wind-up toy fashion, Ivylee handed Momma the leg, and Momma hugged it like a special child she had maybe not seen in years. As gentle as placing a sleeping baby onto a bed, Momma laid the leg onto the sofa until the coffin was properly prepared to her specifications for its odd occupant.

"Maybe Mr. Robinson here could say the blessing. Would you like to do that, Mr. Robinson?"

"Been a long time since I shared a blessing, but yes, I think I would."

"A blessing," Momma recalled. "Ivylee, look out there and see what Precious is doing."

Ivylee looked at Bunk and replied, "He's doing just fine, Momma."

"You do remember Precious, don't you, Mr. Robinson?" Momma asked. "You gave him to us when Ivylee was so sick."

Surprised, Mr. Robinson looked first at me and then at

Momma. "I did?"

"See," Ivylee gloated. "He is not Mr. Robinson. Mr. Robinson would remember a thing like that. He knows every gift he has ever given me."

"It don't take much to remember nothing, Ivylee."

"I don't usually allow my girls to take gifts from men, Mr. Robinson, but since Ivylee was so sick. . ."

"You gave Precious to Ivylee, Momma," I reminded. Confusion was on the rise like dandelions in the summertime, Mr. Robinson was looking a little baffled as he tried to keep up with "who's on first."

"Oh, I don't think so, Sister."

"Trust me on this one, Momma."

"Well, I don't trust either of you anymore. I'd sooner trust a complete stranger than the two of you. So there." Ivylee whirled around to emphasize her point.

"Ivylee, you would believe a cow if it tried to convince you it was a duck." One of the few areas at which Ivylee was adept was ignoring me. She practiced on a regular basis, and with each passing day, she became better at it.

"Before Bunk lost his leg and disappeared, Momma had a purpose didn't you, Momma?" Ivylee asked the question in a tone that suggested she was also trying to understand "who" was on first.

"Suppose I did," Momma answered as she considered Ivylee's reminder, "although I can't seem to recall what it was."

"And Momma always said a person with a purpose can go places, didn't you, Momma?"

"Why, yes, I do believe I did say that. Don't you agree, Mr. Robinson?"

"Would seem so, yes."

"Oh, I just had an idea!" Momma squealed, "Maybe Mr. Robinson here could deliver the eulogy. Would you like to do that, Mr. Robinson? Sister here delivered a beautiful one last week on the mating habits of the worker bee."

"I didn't think the worker bee ever mated?" Mr. Robinson questioned.

"Sister knows all kinds of stuff, although most of it does seem to be a mite useless. She was getting all educated until she had to come home and run the farm."

Unwilling to share center stage, stovetop or not, Ivylee wailed, "It's my turn to deliver the eulogy, and I wrote a special poem. Besides, he obviously didn't even know Bunk."

"Does anybody?" I asked.

"You can recite your poem, Ivylee, and Mr. Robinson here can say the blessing and deliver the eulogy. Oh, this is so exciting! We haven't had company for a service in forever. My, I do love a good time. Don't you, Mr. Robinson?"

"I always say a good time is a good time."

Momma stood still and stared at him like she might be seeing him for the first time. "Why, that's the same thing my Bunk used to say."

"I would consider it a personal favor if the two of you would stop referring to this strange man as Mr. Robinson." Ivylee dropped into the overstuffed chair in hopeless exasperation. The pouty look of frustration on her face suggested she might be going under for the last time.

"Ivylee sure has a sense of humor." Mr. Robinson removed a folded piece of paper and wire-rim glasses from the bib of his overalls.

"It's not a sense of humor Ivylee has," I explained. "It's more a sense of self. It's about all the sense she has."

"I have told you not to talk about me like I'm not here, Sister. And if y'all don't stop referring to this man as Mr.

Robinson, well, I'm just not going to play."

"Speaking of play," Momma recalled, "Ivylee, look out there and see what Precious is doing."

"There's no one out there, Momma. And I wouldn't care what he was doing if he was."

"Ivylee, he has to be out there. That's where I put him. Now let's not keep this up, especially in front of Mr. Robinson. Whatever will he think if you keep carrying on like this?"

"Well, when he comes, we'll ask him," Ivylee announced before she stood and stomped out of the room like she was marching off to glory land.

"And where do you think you're going? We have company."

"Where, Momma? I don't see anybody." Ivylee left the living room in an offended huff.

"Pay no mind to Ivylee," Momma instructed. "I think she's feeling a mite ornery today. But she does love Precious. We all do. He's such a dear, almost like my own, isn't he, Sister?"

"Oh, I think he's more than that, Momma." Turning toward Mr. Robinson I added, "Precious and Momma have gotten to be very close. Not a day goes by that Momma's not out there playing with Precious. It's just touching to see, and every time I see it, I believe I become a little more touched."

Momma meandered across the room to the screen door, as if doing so would help her both understand and explain Precious. "Oh, my, yes. I take Precious to my bosom every day, but sometimes, it don't seem to do no good, and I don't mind saying that some days Precious can be a handful. And you know, sometimes when I look into his eyes, I plain wonder who he is." Momma's voice trailed off like it was taking her to some place else.

The sky had changed from a pastel gray to the husky color of thick smoke. A storm was brewing, and the air was charged with the intensity of it.

"I'm sure he would not want to cause you any concern," Mr. Robinson affirmed in a voice intent on soothing.

"Don't let it worry you too much, Mr. Robinson. Momma loves a good burden."

Momma turned her attention from the view outside the screen door and faced Mr. Robinson. When she did not respond, Mr. Robinson extended a cautious invitation. "I would love to see Precious. Do you think we could get him to come inside for a while?"

"Oh, no. We never let him inside."

"Oh?"

"Precious is a handful, and he might mess things up, and I don't know if I could fix them again."

Mr. Robinson's face reflected a look of concern. He appeared to be keeping a tally in his mind of the game that was being played, and whatever the score, his look suggested he may have lost the last point.

"Momma's really the only one who tries with Precious. For Ivylee, Precious doesn't exist, and I tend to ignore him. As a matter of fact, I tend to ignore them all whenever I can."

Momma fiddled with the unpinned hair at the nape of her neck, and I could sense her agitation as she tried to grope with the subject of this conversation. "Precious is sure full of his mischief though. Before we started bolting the chicken house door, Precious got in there one night." Momma paused as if a warning signal went off in her memory. "Was the same night Bunk left."

In almost a whisper, Mr. Robinson asked, "Really?"

Momma took in a deep breath as though to brace

herself and then turned away from the two of us. "Was a terrible sight what all he did. The next morning, the yard was covered with the bodies of dead chickens." While Momma shared the events of this incident, she seemed to be telling the story more to herself than to us, as though we were not even in the room, or if we were, we were of no more depth or substance than the empty coffin that graced the sideboard.

"Some of them chickens that weren't all the way dead were still jumping around with their wings all spread out and flouncing across the yard with their heads hanging in front of them like a broken handle. It was the most peculiar sight I have ever seen. White chickens laying all over the yard like clumps of soiled clothing and him standing there in the middle of them with a dead chicken in each hand. Through eyes filled with tears, he kept shaking his head and looking like he'd lost something, something sacred, something he surely thought he'd never lose. And Ivylee was sick, so sick she didn't even know her own kin, and Sister was away at that school, and there he was, in the middle of all them dead chickens, screaming 'who, who.'"

The image of this scene was so disturbing that neither Mr. Robinson nor I said anything. Like zombies, we looked on in helpless wonder. To move or speak seemed as though it might violate Momma, and to do so would have surely broken the spell. I think we were both afraid of what might be on the other side. The room was quiet and still, still like the cemetery at dawn.

Momma moved further away from us. "Then there was that awful sound, and there was blood all over them white chickens. Looked like somebody's heart exploded on their wedding dress, somebody's badly broken heart."

For the first time in my life, I was afraid for Momma, and I realized how precariously fragile she truly was. I had taken her presence, her strength, the woman herself for granted. Stepping toward her, I pleaded, "Momma, don't talk about it anymore."

As I placed my arm around her shoulders, Mr. Robinson, whose awkwardness at the moment was even greater than my own, asked, "Can I comfort you any, Momma?"

Momma stared into my eyes as though the question had come from me. "What's done is done. And we just have to live with it. It's what is."

Moving one step closer, Mr. Robinson asked as if planting a seed, "Is it?"

"All that was is gone, and we have Precious. It's just that we don't know what to do with him."

Before anyone could respond, Ivylee entered, crossed to the overstuffed chair and plopped down onto it like dead weight. "I don't like storms. They scare me. Remember how I used to tell you when I was little, Momma, that storms sound like God is mad at us, and you would hold me and say, 'No, Honey, but sometimes we have to be reminded who's in charge.' And then you would sing 'Steal Away' to me." Ivylee looked sideways, as though she could see the words written there and sang in a voice both halting and soft, as soft as candlelight. "'My Lord calls me, He calls me by the thunder. . . My Lord calls me, He calls me by the lightning. . .' Could you tell me that now, Momma?"

Momma just looked at Ivylee like she was trying to remember who Ivylee was. When she said nothing, Mr. Robinson smiled and said, "Yes, sometimes we do have to be reminded who's in charge, don't we?"

The moment was gone, and I was glad. I was concerned for Momma, but I was also anxious to bring her back around to herself. "Living with Precious is sort of like living with a shadow, Mr. Robinson, and there's so many shadows around here that Precious just fuses with the rest of them. After a while, it's hard to tell what's real from what's shadow."

Mr. Robinson cleared his throat. In a voice that sounded awkward and confused as though we spoke in an unknown language, Mr. Robinson responded, "I'm sorry Precious was not more than he was. I wish he could have been more of a comfort."

Mr. Robinson may as well have assaulted Ivylee. He had invaded her space one time too many. "Comfort? Exactly what kind of comfort do you think Precious could bring to anybody? Don't you talk about comfort, you skuzzy, good-for-nothing, slimy, scum-of-the-earth, worm-eating wart! You don't know me. And you ain't gonna get to know me. You are not Mr. Robinson! So there."

"A little hostile, are we, Ivylee?"

Jolted by Ivylee's hostility, Momma's mind came back to her surroundings. "Mind your manners, young lady. You weren't raised to be a beast of the field."

"No, but she's got the jackass part down pat," I offered as I guided Momma to the sofa. "Pay no mind to Ivylee, Mr. Robinson. She gets funny things in her head because there's nothing else up there to fill it up."

As if the girl didn't look goofy enough already, Ivylee stuck her tongue out at me and wiggled her fingers at the side of her head. "Are we going to do the service tonight or not? I'm not going to stick around all night waiting for y'all to get it right."

Although Momma looked weary, more weary than I ever recall seeing her, she tried to interject a light tone of whimsy back into the sound of her voice. "Why, what ever would we do if we didn't do the service?" Before tottering across the room to the coffin, Momma smoothed out the front of her clothes as if doing so would wipe away all the doubt and confusion.

"I been working on my poem, Momma. What do you think of this? 'A merry-go-round eternally bound. . .'"

"That's lovely, dear. Now help us get everything ready for the service."

"But I need to practice my poem."

Momma lit the candles on the end tables while I stirred the baskets of funeral flowers on each end of the sideboard. "You can practice while we get ready, Ivylee. You can recite it over and over, and maybe Bunk's leg will get up and crawl out of here and put an end to all this."

"I wish you weren't here, Sister."

"Just pretend I'm not, then at least one of us will be happy."

Momma removed the leg from the sofa and unwrapped the white butcher paper from around it. "Ivylee, this is not the leg! This is our Sunday dinner. Here. Go put the ham back in the freezer and bring the leg this time."

Momma re-wrapped the ham and thrust it at Ivylee. Had it been any time other than this, I would have probably howled with laughter. As it was, I still sensed Momma's frailty and guarded my sarcastic side like it was a pet rat I kept in a ramshackle cage.

Ivylee snatched the ham out of the air and sashayed out of the living room like she had received some inexcusable insult from the lot of us.

"Ivylee should have been an actress," Mr. Robinson pointed out.

"Oh, she is. She acts every day. The only role she doesn't act is intelligent."

"Unkind words can rob you, Sister."

"Then consider me one of the long-suffering poor."

With a pencil and journal poised in her hands, Momma

160

asked, "Sister, do you have anything you want to say tonight?"

"I'll pass."

"In that case, it will be Mr. Robinson and Ivylee on the program."

Still sashaying as though swinging her hips would whisk away her cares, Ivylee pranced back into the living room and presented Momma with the leg.

Momma unwrapped the butcher paper from around Bunk's leg and removed a blue baby blanket from inside a drawer in the sideboard. A large "S" had been embroidered in the middle of the blanket. Momma draped the Superman blanket about the leg and eased it inside the coffin.

Curious as to how this was playing to Mr. Robinson, I glanced in his direction and was surprised to see a sense of peace upon his face.

Momma took her place at one end of the sofa while I took my place at the other. "Ivylee, are you going to sit in the balcony tonight?"

"Can I go first, Momma?"

"Mr. Robinson should pray first."

"Then I'll sit in the balcony." Ivylee stomped across the room, stepped up onto the sofa seat, twirled around, and sat down on the back of the sofa.

"Mr. Robinson?"

Mr. Robinson looked up to the ceiling, cleared his throat and lowered his head. "'There is none holy as the Lord: for there is none beside thee: neither is there any rock like our God.'" Mr. Robinson lifted his head and glanced at Momma.

"That was lovely, Mr. Robinson. Did you write it yourself?"

"No, it was given to me."

From the opposite end of the sofa, I watched as

Momma and Mr. Robinson exchanged looks.

Apparently frustrated that she was not the center of attention, Ivylee stood and demanded, "Is it my turn yet?"

"What?" Momma answered in a startled voice.

"Is it my turn yet?"

"Yes, yes, go ahead."

Ivylee stepped down from her seat in the balcony, sauntered over to the old stove where she removed a play circus baton and hat from inside the oven. With the hat donned atop her head, she stepped onto the oven door and then onto the top of the stove. "'Yesterday and the Day Before,' by Ivylee. 'Life is a carousel with pigs and possums, birds and blossoms, horses galore and so much more; Death is a carousel, going round and round and up and down with empty sounds—a merry-go-round eternally bound to a clock, stopped in the belly of a bird; As we wait for Life, And we wait for Death, And we wait. . .'" Looking like a tattered Shirley Temple doll that had overdosed on cold medicine, Ivylee stopped abruptly, smiled, and curtsied.

Momma clapped with proud vigor. "That was beautiful, Ivylee."

Mr. Robinson followed Momma's lead, clapping and nodding his head. "Yes, it was."

"That was the stupidest thing I have ever heard."

"Sister."

"Well, it was."

"You apologize to your sister right this minute. She's been working on that poem since forever, and it was lovely. Now you tell her so or we'll go through the whole thing all over again."

Momma glared at me while waiting for her child to do the right thing. "That was indeed a masterful rendition of poetic license if I ever heard one, Ivylee."

"What?" the ninny asked.

"Your poem is like you, unique in an off-the-wall sort of way."

"I knew you'd like it." Grinning like she had discovered a long, lost love, Ivylee stepped down from the stove and returned to her seat in the balcony.

"Sister, why don't you lead us in a song? That way you can participate in the program too."

"Oh, wonderful," I replied with about as much excitement as I would have at the prospect of gutting a chicken. I could have whined and complained and even refused, but I knew from past experience that I would lose. Begrudgingly, I stood and with no more feeling than slopping hogs, I sang, "'. . .There is pow'r, pow'r, wonder-working pow'r in the blood of the Lamb. There is pow'r, pow'r, wonder-working pow'r in the precious blood of the Lamb.'"

Startled, Momma looked like I had slapped her across the face. The fear trapped in Momma's eyes suggested I had somehow shared her darkest secret, and an alarm went off in my head that left me feeling vulnerable. "Are you all right, Momma? Where are your pills?" Before I could get to her, a sudden boom of thunder seemed to roll right through the house. The power went out, and except for the candles, we were in an eerie, unsettling darkness. Lightning flashed with such intensity that it hurt our eyes, and for a few seconds, the living room would be lit as though from a yellow bug light.

In one swift movement, Ivylee jumped behind the sofa. "What was that?"

"Power's off."

In a voice that seemed to be far away, Momma murmured, "Power went off the same day Bunk went away."

"Just stay put, Momma. I'll find a flashlight." I moved cautiously across the room to the coat rack by the door, where a flashlight hung from one of the wooden knobs.

In the glow of the flashlight, before climbing back onto her seat, Ivylee peeked over the top of the sofa like a frightened soldier from a foxhole. Her circus hat had fallen onto the floor, and she stood on the sofa holding the baton in such a way as to suggest she might take aim at any moment. When another boom of thunder shook the house, Ivylee held the baton as though to shield her eyes from enemy fire. With the next flash of lightning, the shadow of Ivylee on the back of the living room wall looked like the image of a woman holding a gun.

In the eeriness of the moment, Momma snapped to attention, and in a voice so shrill it seemed to pierce the darkness, she cried, "I did it. I did it! The blood's on me."

Another voice, one that I had not heard in a long time, softly countered, "No, it's not, Momma."

"Are you all right, Momma? Do you have your pills?"

Like a puppet hanging from loose strings, Ivylee stood on the sofa. "I call this one 'Power Failure,' Momma. 'Is God there when the lights go out? Is He there when eyes close? Does He hear whispers in the dark? Whispers evaporate like vapor. Do they reach their destination? Is God there when the lights go out? In darkness where emptiness surrounds like a shroud.' What'd ya think of that one, Momma?"

"Ivylee, will you sit down and shut-up? Are you okay, Momma? What do you mean there's blood on you? Have you hurt yourself?"

"Oh, dear, God," Momma moaned, "I did it."

With my voice expressing more concern than curiosity and with the fear that Momma might give in to whatever it was that was happening inside her head, I begged,

"Momma, please, don't."

"*I* shot Bunk's leg off! It was me. I did it."

"You're just confused, Momma. It's been a long day." We had never known for certain how Bunk lost his leg and had assumed it happened while he was cleaning his gun. All Momma had ever said was that it was an accident.

That voice from another time rejoined, "It's okay. It doesn't matter anymore." When the power came back on, he stood next to Momma with his arm around her shoulders.

"Where are your heart pills?" I searched her pockets and removed a small brown bottle of nitroglycerin tablets. "Here, put this under your tongue."

Momma's glazed eyes stared straight ahead, apparently reading a memory, and although I doubted she knew who I was at that moment, Momma followed my instruction.

With his arm about her, he spoke to her with such softness in his voice as to suggest he feared words might break her. "Is there anything I can do for you, Momma?"

"Was my fault," she cried.

"No, it wasn't."

"We wouldn't be here tonight if it wasn't for me." Momma moved away from the two of us and drifted like an apparition across the room to the coffin. "And Bunk wouldn't be in this sorry state if. . ."

"Please, don't," he pleaded.

Scared, like she was afraid any noise would cause our house to cave in, Ivylee murmured, "What is she talking about?"

Standing in front of the coffin, Momma closed her eyes. "It wasn't his fault that preacher robbed me of my cherry in the chicken house."

Like a wounded warrior come home from the war, he limped across the room to be next to her. "Don't," he whispered as he lifted her chin and looked into her eyes. "You don't have to."

Unable to sustain neither a thought nor an emotion for more than a brief moment, Ivylee screeched like a cat caught in a rainstorm, "And where did you get cherries? I haven't had any cherries."

Glaring at Ivylee as though I could cut her with my eyes, through clinched teeth, I muttered, "She's not talking about those kind of cherries, Ivylee."

"Oh? Oh, my!"

"That preacher had no business doing what he did, and I had no business telling Bunk. I should have buried it, buried it in a place so deep that even death couldn't claim it."

"Then bury it now," he whispered.

Through the years, we had heard only bits and pieces of stories from Momma's youth, but we had never heard any part of this, and as I watched, I wasn't sure I wanted to hear it. "He's right, Momma. You don't have to tell this."

"Might make her feel better to tell it."

"Shut-up, Ivylee."

Although Momma stood before us, shared the same room, she was some place else, at a scene in her mind from another time. "Was the fall I turned fourteen. My Momma and Papa had left word for the preacher to come talk to me about getting married because I didn't want to, but Papa couldn't afford to feed me no more. Winter was coming on, and the summer crops had not been good, and there wasn't even enough money for coal to heat the house in the months ahead. We didn't have much and what we had mostly belonged to somebody else. Papa was just doing the best he could with what he had."

We all stood still like chess pieces waiting to be moved to the next square.

"On the day that preacher came, Momma made me put on my Sunday dress, the white one with the pink roses on the hem, the one I was to get married in. Papa was feeling poorly that day, so he sent me to raise the curtains in the chicken house, so the evening chill wouldn't fall on them. Papa always took good care of his chickens." Momma paused as though to consider the comment.

"Our preacher had moved on to another church, so we didn't have our regular one. The one that came was a circuit preacher, nobody we knew. Momma and Papa told him I'd gone out to the chicken house, so he came out there. When he stepped inside the door, he didn't say anything, just watched me while I raised the curtains and hooked them on the nails above the windows, his dark suit collecting dust where he stood.

"When I finished hooking the last curtain, he turned and propped his Bible on the ledge above the door. Then he came over to where I was standing, and he placed his big hands on my shoulders and turned me toward him. Clutching my arms, he stood firm in front of me like he was the pulpit and me the altar. 'Sister,' he said, 'your ma and pa wants me to prepare you for marryin', so here I be to do it. Marrying is serious business, Sister, so we need somewhere where we can talk serious. How 'bout that feed bin over there?' Seemed an odd thing, but nobody had ever talked to me about marrying before, and he was a preacher, so I didn't question. Wasn't my place.

"Like a little lamb, I followed him through the chicken house, and white chickens with angel wings flew in front of him, flew in frightened frenzy. At the feed bin, he climbed the ladder, and when he reached the ledge, he turned and motioned to me. He grabbed my hand and pulled me in on top of him. And in that feed bin, in the darkness of that wooden box, he groped for me, put his big hands on me, and pushed me down into the chicken feed. And I whispered prayers in the blackness, prayed the feed would swallow me in its depth. While the chicken feed moved and shifted like quicksand beneath our weight, he lifted my dress, ripped my slip, and pulled at my panties like I was a house-warming present he was about to open. He lowered his large self on me, came down on top of me, until I couldn't breathe, and I drown in the darkness of his might, and he was heavy and dark and dusty. 'From dust to dust.' From dark to darkness. And I drowned in his darkness. I gasped, but no sound came out. Papa couldn't hear me, couldn't take care of his chickens. The only sounds in the thick musky darkness of that feed bin was his heavy breathing and the chickens that shuffled about beneath us. That preacher thrust himself upon me, and screams from deep inside myself were smothered by his might—'*he was a man of God.*' And his darkness penetrated me, and I closed my eyes and died for a while." Momma paused, hesitated like she feared what came next. "And in the darkness of the feed bin, that preacher prepared me."

Tears streaked down her cheeks while we all stood there helpless to help her, the shock on each of our faces a reflection of the other's.

"When he finished, there was blood on my dress, blood on my wedding dress." Momma closed her eyes, swallowed hard as she appeared to grapple with the words. "He said it was the blood of Christ, said it was on all of us."

The room was still, as still as an empty well. No one knew what to say or even if they should move. Her pain was such that to do so might hurt her even more. The story had cast its spell of shame on all of us, and we all stood and stared at each other like we had been caught playing some cruel, forbidden game of statutes with fear frozen on our stone faces.

When neither Ivylee nor I could find any words, the voice of long ago tiptoed into our present and begged to be heard. "He was wrong, all wrong."

"The day I married, I learned his name, one I would carry with me." Momma leaned over the coffin, and through choked tears whispered, "I'm so sorry, Bunk." She lowered the lid of the coffin like she had closed some part of her life, and in front of the closed coffin, she cited, "'Ask, and it shall be given you; seek and ye shall find; knock, and it shall be opened unto you. . .'" With her head bowed and her shoulders slumped, her voice quivered as though it feared its own response. "I did. I did, but no one was there."

"Yes, there was," he whispered.

Tears filled my eyes, and the room was as still and cold as an icebox. Like a scream from a nightmare, a siren blared along the road beyond the house, and the abruptness of the piercing sound startled us all to life.

Confused, Momma ran to the door and looked out. "Wonder who it is this time. You think it's for me?" With a look of frightened anticipation, she turned to me, "What time shall we go to the parlor tomorrow?"

Fear raced through me as I rushed to her side and placed my arm around her small shoulders. "I don't think we should go to the parlor tomorrow, Momma. I think you should rest."

"I have to see who's there. It might be me."

While I fought back tears, he moved slowly to her other side, as if between the two of us, we could shield and protect her. "You're not going to find what you're looking for there, Momma."

Momma looked at him like she was surprised to see him. "I don't think I know what you're saying. Now who are you?"

Ivylee, whose fear at one point could have mirrored Momma's, had now mustered enough courage to react. "He said he was Mr. Robinson, but he's not."

"Do you believe it, Sister?"

"If you want me to, Momma."

Looking for any excuse to leave the room, Ivylee stood with her hands on her hips. "Well, I won't. And I'm going to bed." Momma had trained Ivylee so well in the use of make believe that I often wondered if Ivylee considered herself real at all, or if in her own mind, she was some pretend person, an illusion in someone else's fantasy.

"Don't you think you should see about Precious first, Ivylee?"

"Precious," Ivylee repeated as she pointed toward Mr. Robinson. "Why don't you let him see about Precious? He seems to be so taken with him."

"But he might not know Precious."

"Well, neither do I." Ivylee marched out of the living room like a band of discomfited troops was following her. In her room, I knew she would hide under the covers, where in her fetal position, she would no doubt pray that reality would not get her.

In a reassuring voice, he begged, "I'd be happy to take care of everything for you, Momma."

"Do I know you?" Puzzled, Momma looked first at him and then at me.

"Come on, Momma. Let's get you to bed."

"It has been a long day, hasn't it? Everything will be back like it was tomorrow. Don't you think so?"

"Yes, Momma. I'm sure it will."

Momma paused and looked at me like awareness of who I was had just come back to her. "I'm sorry, Sister."

"Let's not talk about it anymore."

As we moved slowly toward the hall door, Momma

stopped again. "What about? What's his name?"

"Mr. Robinson," I replied.

"What about Mr. Robinson?"

"Don't worry about me, Momma. I make myself at home wherever I am."

"Oh. In that case, good night."

"And good night to you, lovely lady."

Bewildered, Momma again looked at him and then at me. With a cautious smile, she said, "He is precious, isn't he?"

While I guided Momma slowly toward the hall, he turned and stepped out onto the front porch. I watched him through the screen door as he paused to study the doorknob nestled among the roots of the tree stump, and I wondered who would be here tomorrow.

Chapter 15

Knock, Knock

When I put Momma to bed that night, I sat beside her until she drifted off to needed sleep, a sleep that was anything but restful. Watching her chest rise and fall with each heavy breath, she tossed, turned and repeatedly shook her head, as if to shake memories or dreams loose from their chokehold on her.

Sitting beside Momma's bed, I considered our lives, considered how long life sometimes seemed, when in truth how short it really was. I had never been a particularly spiritual person. My spiritual beliefs were probably more convenience than anything else. For me, it was simply easier to believe than not to believe. I considered faith to be much like having an insurance policy, decided early on I would rather live my life *believing* with the looming possibility of finding out at death's sting that there was no God than to live my life *not believing* and find out at the end that there was one. This rationalization was how I paid my insurance premiums. Believing left me with nothing to prove outside myself, and outside myself was where I tried to reside. Besides, Momma seemed to believe enough for all of us, which I guess I felt as her offspring would extend to me in that her beliefs would in some way validate my ticket and maybe pay for my sins.

As I sat beside the bed of the person who had had the greatest influence on my life, I considered that a day would come, and possibly sooner than I thought, when that influence would no longer be present in a physical state. A fear rose inside me that I had either never felt or had kept at bay, and that fear began to twist and turn in me like a jagged dagger snagging on all my unsecured parts. While I gazed upon the form of this fragile person who lay at rest before me, for the first time, I considered her mortality.

Despite her peculiarities and any questions as to her actions, her tender heart was always in the right place. I could not say the same for myself. The sarcastic, bitter person I had allowed myself to become was no one I ever intended to be. I walked by sight alone; Momma walked by faith. Even though her faith did not necessarily come with understanding, she truly received "the kingdom of God as a little child."

Tears floated across my eyes, and as quietly as I could, I moved from my chair to the floor beside her bed where I bowed my head and whispered prayers into my cupped hands, prayers sent up in earnest as my Mother's child. When I finished my prayers, my fear of how precariously close we were to possibly losing Momma would not let me leave her. From the closet in her room, I removed several quilts and made a pallet on the far side of her bed next to the window. Exhausted, I fell into a deep sleep.

In the pre-dawn hours, our sleep was interrupted by a knock on the bedroom door. Confused, I tried to place the knock on the door into my dream and did not respond.

When neither Momma nor I answered, the knock came again. Although I sensed Momma's movement on the bed as she lifted herself to a sitting position, I could not tell if she was once again frozen at what presence she feared might be on the other side. Before I could wake and rouse myself enough to respond, Momma asked in a voice that suggested calm resignation, "Who's there?"

From the other side of the door, a voice whispered, "May I come in?"

"I don't feel like company right now."

The door opened, and a reassuring voice responded, "It's just me. I'd like to talk to you. So may I please come in?"

The bed springs squeaked and groaned as Momma adjusted the pillow against the headboard and leaned back. Pulling the covers across her, she answered, "If you feel you must."

"Didn't you hear me knocking?"

"Didn't expect anybody to be there. Never has been."

"Yes, there was." Across the floor underneath the bed, I could see him amble across the room. He sat down in the chair beside her bed, and as he did, a thin, yellow, hardback book fell to the floor.

"There was?" Momma asked.

"Yes. Always has been. He knocks, but He can't open the door for us. Each of us must open it for our self."

"But you never know who might be on the other side. Might be Satan," Momma warned.

"Satan cannot live in a heart that is full, that has no vacancy." I watched as his hand reached down to pick up the yellow book.

"Mr. Robinson?" Momma asked with suspicion punctuating the question.

174

"No."

"You a Bible salesman?" As I listened, she removed her large black Bible from the nightstand. "I already have a Bible. Mine's a red-letter edition too. See."

"I'm not selling Bibles. I'm not selling anything." He paused. "I've come to help you find God."

All was quiet for a moment before Momma asked in a halting voice, "Am I about to die?"

"No."

Momma released a sigh that sounded as though it came more from her heart and mind than from any place else.

"You're going to live in the light of the Lord."

Propping my head on my elbow for a better view, I waited as Momma replaced the Bible on the nightstand and removed a glass of water I had left there. I listened as she took a sip of water and replaced the glass on the nightstand. "Won't that make it hard to sleep?"

"You sleep the sleep of death already."

"I do? And I didn't even know it. Maybe you could sell Sister a Bible. All she has is a children's Bible, and I think she may have outgrown it."

As if she had said nothing, he continued, "You walk around in a world of darkness like a blind person who doesn't know she can't see."

"Do you have any holy water? I always wanted some holy water. Tell me, what is it exactly that they do with holy water? Do they bathe in it? Or do they just dab some behind their ears? Does that mean they can hear God better? Yes, I definitely want me some of that holy water. My hearing is not nigh what it used to be."

"I don't have any holy water."

"You don't? Then what you got? You got any little crosses? Ivylee's birthday is coming up, and she'd probably love a little cross."

175

"What I got is The Word."

"You don't say. Where'd you get it?"

"I was sitting under a tree, reading this book when it came to me."

Momma took the book, opened it, and as I listened, I could hear her turn page after page. With curious fascination, she asked, "Well, isn't that nice? And you got it from this book? I get mine from The Bible."

While Momma continued with her evaluation of the book, he explained, "The way I see it is like this. Life is this huge puzzle that we spend all our days trying to put together, only to find out when we're done that there's a piece missing, and that the monkey we been carrying around on our back has eaten the missing piece. So we can either operate on the monkey, and possibly do him in, or we can just leave the space empty, glaring at us every day for the rest of our life. And even if we got the piece back, most likely it wouldn't fit anymore. So all-in-all, what we're left with is either an empty space or a piece that doesn't fit."

When Momma did not respond, he stood and sat down on the bed beside her. "And we won't know any peace until we know this." He paused, and as I peered over the edge of the bed, Momma appeared to be studying his face. "So see, we had it all along, the missing piece, that is." When Momma still did not respond, he added, "That's the word I got. It was sort of given to me, like a gift, and I want to give it to you."

"Oh, I don't think you should do that. It ain't polite. I know it would hurt my feelings awful bad if I gave you a gift, and you just gave it away. Grandmother Stamps used to do that. You would give her something, and the next thing you knew, she would go and give it to the next person to come along. When I was little, I remember this confused

176

me, and it made me wonder who she was, if she was really my grandmother."

"But some gifts get better if you give them away," he asked. "What if it's that kind of gift?"

"You'll have to let me think about that one."

"And what if somebody else needs it more?"

I could hear the gentle tapping of Momma's fingers against her lips. "That's a tough one."

"Let me put it this way then. If you don't listen, you don't hear; and if you don't look, you don't see; and if you don't feel, you don't hurt. Isn't that what you believe?"

Momma sighed as she closed the little, yellow book and laid it aside. "I don't rightly know what I believe anymore. It's all gotten to be more than I can understand. Is that what you believe?"

"No, it's not."

"No? Well, then I won't believe it either. If you're not a Bible salesman and if you're not Mr. Robinson, then who are you? Are you a man of God?"

"There are no men of God. There are men, and there *is* God."

Silence seemed to fill the room like thick smoke, and even from where I was, I sensed Momma staring at him. "Well, then are you my new meter reader? We seem to have lost our other one."

"You know who I am, Momma."

"Sister said you were Mr. Robinson."

"Yes, she did. I didn't think you would let me come in otherwise. The door's been closed for a long time."

The tone of her voice echoed uncertainty and trepidation. "Have you come back for your leg?"

"Don't need my leg to be made whole. Besides, that's not my leg anymore."

As though to catch him in a lie, Momma asked, "Then

177

whose is it?"

"It's not anybody's leg anymore. It's only a reminder."

"If you're Bunk, that's your leg."

"It was once, but not anymore. It's your leg now."

The bed squeaked as Momma pulled her head back to look at him like he might be infectious. As I peeked over the edge of the bed, I had to catch myself to keep from snickering. "But that can't be. I got all my legs. See." Momma threw the covers from across her legs.

"It was my leg once," he said, "but I don't need it anymore, so it's not my leg. It's your leg now because you're using it, sort of like a crutch."

"Whether you need it or not, it's your leg," Momma insisted. "And I got both my legs, and if I got two good legs, what do I need a crutch for? The only people who need a crutch are cripples, and I'm not a cripple. See." Momma slipped out of bed and walked around the room to demonstrate.

"It's not that kind of crutch. It's a crutch you use to get by."

"Well, what good is a crutch, if you don't use it for walking, especially if it's a leg? That makes no sense at all. I surely hope you can do better than this after all this time."

There was a long pause, as the two of them appeared to be sizing up the situation as well as each other. "Momma, let's bury the leg."

"Bury the leg? But what'll I use for a coffee table?"

"We can make do."

"We? We who?"

"Me and you."

"Me and you," Momma repeated. "I don't even know who you are."

"Yes, you do."

"But you said that leg out there wasn't yours, and that's

Bunk's leg out there, so you must not be Bunk. And besides, I don't know that I could trust somebody who won't even claim their own leg."

"The leg is mine, Momma."

"I knew it!"

"But I don't need it anymore," he explained. "You've been using it, so it's kind of become yours."

"We already been through this. Wait a minute. I'll be right back." Momma left the bedroom, and while I lowered myself back onto the pallet, I could hear her pattering down the hall to the living room. Moments later, she returned singing as she came down the hall. "'Rock-a-bye baby in the tree top, When the wind blows, the cradle will rock. . .'" When I peered over the top of the bed, I watched as she removed the blanket from around the leg and held it up. "See. This is your leg. And see these overalls, these are your overalls. I don't wear overalls. Never have. Unsightly for a lady of the house to wear overalls. Not only that, but they're the darndest nuisance when you have to go to the bathroom. And see?" Momma knocked gently on both Bunk's legs to discern which was the artificial one. Holding the leg in place where it once would have been, she added, "This leg goes right here. Except it used to be a little bigger. Guess I should have exercised it more."

"Momma, I know the leg is mine."

"Now we're getting some place."

"But since I don't need it anymore and haven't in some time, it's sort of yours now. I guess you could say I gave it to you."

"Oh, I see." Momma paused as she appeared to consider this. "Sort of like I gave Mr. Robinson to Ivylee."

"Sort of."

"Because she needed something." Again, Momma paused as though to think about what he had said. "Except

Mr. Robinson wasn't real, and this leg is real. It is real, isn't it?"

"What's real doesn't matter. It's what you believe that matters. Every day of your life is real, but it's your beliefs that get you through."

Cradling the leg in her arms, Momma sat down on the side of the bed. "I don't think I understand."

"Okay," he said. "I guess what I'm saying is that you have to be like a, like a morning glory, and try every day to bloom bright and beautiful, even among the weeds if you have to."

"But morning glories are a bind weed. Are you telling me I need to be a weed?"

"Well, yes, I guess I am," he chuckled. "Even if you start out as a weed, you could bloom into something beautiful. It's sorta like this. When we're first born, we're totally open like a flower, like a morning glory at morning's light. We're all open and beautiful and flourish in the light. But as the day goes on, and the light starts to wane, we begin to close. We start to feel vulnerable, so we turn away from the light. And before long, we begin to tell ourselves we don't need the light. Sometimes we even try to convince ourselves the light is not really there, and we begin to look for things to fill the void the light left, because the darkness is so permeating. And what we live soon becomes what we believe, and we begin to convince ourselves that we're 'it' in the universe, the big 'M' and the big 'E,' the mighty 'ME.' Because we think we're in control, it is so much easier to believe in our self than to believe beyond our self. Believing makes demands on us; not believing asks nothing of us. So we spend our lives playing this game, but when the game is over, if we're still 'it,' we lose."

Momma's voice was hesitant like she was afraid of the

answer, "Did we lose?"

"No, we're still in the game, but we gotta get off the sidelines." He sat on the bed beside her. Peeking over the side, I watched as he took her hand. "It all comes down to this. You remember the story of the farmer who sowed the seeds?"

"From the Bible, yes, and I always thought he was rather careless to be dropping his seeds every place."

"Well, yes, but that's just it. That's the point. Seeds were scattered in different places, but none of ours took root. I was like the seed that fell among the thorns, and I let the worries of this world choke my beliefs out of me. And you were like the seed that didn't understand, and so it got snatched away from you."

As though she were trying to solve a math problem, Momma appeared to be thinking about what he had said. "What about Ivylee? What kind of seed is she?"

"Well, I haven't figured that one out yet, but I'm working on it."

I had to place my hand over my mouth to keep from laughing out loud. Had I not been hiding and eavesdropping, I would have added that Ivylee is probably like hydro seeding. Her seed was mixed and sprayed, but never landed anywhere and just floats in air.

For a couple of moments, the two of them were so quiet that I peeked over the edge to see what was going on and saw him brush a wisp of hair away from her face.

"Momma, I am so sorry about it all. When I learned that my father had raped you, something inside me just broke, something that had served as my safe place just broke into. The man who throughout my life I had seen as an apostle was only a flawed man, a man who in one moment forsake everything—his faith, his ministry, his family. His whole life was a lie. And if his life was a lie and my life was based on his, then mine must have been a lie too. And so like him, I forsake everything."

Curious as to what Momma would do, I continued to peek over the top of the bed. She looked down to the hand that was wrapped around hers, and in a voice as tender as a mother's to a hurting child, she said, "No, you just got lost for a little while."

"All those years, I thought I had been taking care of you, and come to find out you were taking care of me. I felt so helpless. There are some things in life you simply want to believe, and when they start to crumble, your foundation can give way right out from under you. Either that or you find out you had no foundation at all. The man I'd modeled my entire life after was a fraud. And if he was, then what did that make me?"

"But you're not your father," Momma whispered.

"I know that now. Blood may bind us together, but it doesn't define who we are. Who I am is who I choose to be and who I am now is also where I am now, and where I am is with you, that is, if you'll have me." Lowering my head onto my elbow, I saw his good leg shake while he waited for her response, and it tore at my heart.

"I'm so sorry. I should never have told you. I never intended to. It's just that when Ivylee got so sick, and you said you would call your father to come pray over her, it scared me so bad. She was so frail, and I. . ."

"Don't," he interrupted. "You don't have to explain. You don't ever have to explain." When he paused, I peered over the edge of the bed again and watched as he cupped his hand to her cheek. "Your love made me Precious. Don't apologize for it. Any apologies are mine and should come solely from me. And I am so sorry."

She was quiet, and I sensed she might be fighting back the tears that had wanted to come for so long. Then as if to make him feel better, she added, "Oh, it's okay. We all have our bad days."

"And some days seem to go on forever." In a voice soft with pleading, he asked, "So can I come back?"

To my surprise, Momma turned her attention to the leg and sang, "'. . .When the bough breaks, the cradle will fall, And down will come baby cradle and all.'" She laid the leg on the bed beside her and gently covered it. "I just want you to know I never meant to shoot you." With a halting sound of caution in her voice as if she were trying to brace herself not to cry, she added, "I closed my eyes when the gun went off."

"I know that." Silence hung awkwardly in the air for a moment before he added, "I'm just grateful it wasn't a cannon."

Momma giggled like a schoolgirl, and I watched as he leaned forward and kissed her on the cheek, kissed her gently as though it were their first kiss.

"Oh, my precious Bunk," she whispered. Momma laid her head upon his shoulder, and he wrapped his arm around her.

Pulling his head back from her slightly, he gazed onto her face. "Why didn't you put me away?"

"Because you were mine, and because I had to believe one day you would be back. I had to have that. If I didn't have that, I didn't have anything."

"Yes, you did." Bunk removed Momma's Bible from the nightstand, turned a few pages to a marked passage and read, "'And he was clothed with a vesture dipped in blood: and his name is called the Word of God.' We both did. He's been here all along." Bunk closed the Bible and placed it on the nightstand.

"He's here? He's really here? Oh, dear, and I'm not even dressed. Where is He? Is He on the front porch?"

With their fingers interlocked, Bunk pointed first to his heart and then to Momma's. "He's here, Momma, here in our hearts. It's what I was trying to tell you before."

"Oh, I thought maybe He was coming to 'sup.'"

Bunk smiled, "Maybe another time."

"You sure I'm not gonna die? I mean if you got God with you and all."

Bunk lifted Momma's face to his. "God turned the light back on for me, and He sent me here to turn it on for you."

"Ain't that nice? The switch is right over there. Or you think He'd prefer this lamp?" I could not help but chuckle to myself as I watched Momma motion to the lamp beside her bed.

"It's not that kind of light. It's like '. . .I am the light of the world: he that followeth me shall not walk in darkness but shall have the light of life.' It's that kind of light, Momma. You and me, well, we've been dwelling in the valley of the shadow of death."

"But I can't afford to move, Bunk. And besides, I like it here. Wait a minute. I thought this was 'Robin's Rest.'"

Bunk ambled across the room to the closet where he removed a white, floor-length nightgown. "Momma, what is this?"

Momma answered hesitantly, "It's a gown." Tilting her head from side-to-side like a young bird fascinated by its reflection, she added, "I hope we're not going to have to go through this with everything, Bunk. That could tax my patience a mite."

"What kind of gown?"

"The one I'm to be buried in."

"How long have you had it?"

"Oh, I don't know, a long time."

"You've been waiting to die for a long time, Momma."

"Well, after I shot you, I didn't know what to expect.

Figured God was pretty upset with me, and I best be prepared."

Bunk handed the gown to Momma. "Here, put it on."

Momma took the gown, but suspicion seemed to creep into her voice. "Whatever for? You not going to bury me, are you?"

"Of course not."

"I think I'd like to die before I'm buried. That's the way it usually goes, you know."

"Remember? I said I was going to turn the light on for you."

With sweet surprise, Momma asked, "I have to get dressed for you to do that? I never realized you were so modest, Bunk."

"It's not that kind of light. Remember? So please put the gown on."

"But why? It's still dark outside, and I already got on a nightgown. See?"

"Because we have something we have to do."

"Right now? At this hour?"

"Yes."

Momma took the gown and went behind the screen that sat in the far corner of the room to change. "What we gonna do? Is it a secret?"

"We're going to bury the leg!"

"In the wee hours of the morning?"

"What better time?"

"A sunrise service! Oh, how wonderful!" Momma stepped from behind the screen. Laying on my belly and peeking around the foot of the bed, I looked on in complete wonder as to how this would play out. With her white hair hanging loosely about her shoulders, Momma looked wildly radiant. "I'm ready. Let's do it. Let's bury the leg. Just let me do my hair."

As Momma began to move across the room to the mirror that hung on the back of the closet door, Bunk stepped in front of her. "No, don't. You look lovely." From where I crouched, I could see him cup her face in his hands. "More lovely than I remembered."

I was guessing Momma's pale face flushed a warm pink. "Oh, Bunk, I'll declare. You're going to make me plum giddy carrying on like that."

Although I felt guilty to be watching, I certainly could not leave at this moment, and I was completely fascinated by what was going on between the two of them.

Holding her in his arms, Bunk leaned forward, and kissed her hair. "Thank you for holding it together while a part of me was so far away."

"Just made do. Sometimes, all you can do is make do." Even in the dim light, I could see a lone tear glisten and roll down her cheek to disappear onto her gown. "I've missed you so, Bunk."

Bunk wiped the trail of the tear from her cheek with his thumb and kissed the woman who had loved him both whole and in part, and whose heart had belonged to him since the day they said, "I do."

"I've missed me too," Bunk teased. Locked in the security of each other's arms, they both laughed.

"Why didn't you come in before?"

"When my senses left me, they must have taken everything else with them, even God. I couldn't find Him, and without him, I guess I couldn't find myself either, and I didn't know how to live my life anymore." Before Momma could ask, Bunk explained. "I slipped in the pond, hit my head, and almost drowned. My life didn't flash before my eyes, but all the empty places in it did, and what I saw startled me, and it startled me enough to shake me loose from whatever had its hold on me. Some odd state of amnesia had eaten the last years of my life, and I wasn't going to let it claim any more of it. I had been lost for so long that it took me a while to piece it all back together. I had to almost die to realize life, my life, our life."

Momma placed the palm of her hand against Bunk's cheek. "My dear Bunk, you're my life."

"That's nice, but it's not true. Life matters while we're living it, but what truly matters is what comes after. Somewhere out there, I caught a glimpse of that, a light that swept me up and turned me around. I don't understand it all, but we got time to figure it out, and we'll make the most of what is, and what is for us, is now."

"Oh, Bunk, you say such pretty things." Momma sighed as if to collect herself. "And we've never had a sunrise service before. It's gonna be such fun. Can we have candles? Be like a birthday, your birthday, Bunk."

"Our birthday. Candles it is."

"Oh, how sweet, but where shall we bury it?" Momma paused to consider the options. "It's your call, Bunk. I mean, after all it is your leg."

"Yes, but it's meant more to you of recent. You decide where you want it buried."

"How about beside the barn? In front of the Robin's Rest sign."

"Perfect," Bunk agreed.

"Okay, then that's where we'll put it. You go dig the grave, and I'll wake the girls, and get everything ready."

As I crouched around the edge of the bed, I saw Momma take Bunk by the hand, as the two of them were making their way to the door. "You sure you want to go through with this?"

"I'm sure. Are you sure?"

With only the slightest hint of doubt, Momma answered, "I think so, although I am kind of attached to it."

"You can attach to me."

"Oh, Bunk, if you ain't a sight." Momma giggled like the young girl she once was. "But, Bunk, one thing has to be clear. The head stone has got to read, 'Here Lies Bunk's Leg.' Otherwise, it's going to be awful confusing."

Bunk chuckled. "Whatever you say."

Just down the hall, Momma stopped and scurried back to the bedroom as I scurried back to crouching at the end of the bed. "Oh, my, we almost forgot the leg." She scooped the leg up and into her arms and cradled it like the baby it had become to her. "Come on, sweetie pea. We're going to have a little party for you."

Momma walked beside Bunk cradling the bundle that had held her life for so long. While I lingered at the door and watched, the two of them moved cautiously into the living room where Momma turned on the light.

"You know where the shovel is, and the flashlight's over there." Momma pointed in the direction of the coat rack.

Bunk kissed Momma on the cheek. "Then let's get on with it." From the darkness of the hall, I watched as he made his way across the room. When his hand came to rest on the doorknob on the front door, he turned his head toward Momma and grinned. "I'll be back." Even from where I stood, I could see the sparkle in his eyes, eyes that had been dull and empty for so long, now sparkled with life.

Momma's face appeared to glow as she watched the man she had married so many years before remove the flashlight dangling from the coat rack and amble slowly out the door. She watched and waited, and to her, he *was,* without a doubt, what he had always been, precious.

Chapter 16

Remember

Secretly, I followed the two of them to the living room, curious beyond belief as to how this would all play out. As I peeked around the hall door, to my surprise, I was as excited as a kid on Christmas morning.

Momma stood at the screen door watching Bunk shuffle down the steps. "Bunk?"

"Yes."

"Oh, nothing. I just wanted to hear you answer."

"Get ready," I heard him say. "We have a lot of time to make up."

Momma nodded her head in sweet affirmation. When he was out of sight, she turned and placed the leg on the sofa. "Now, Sweetie, you sit right here and just take it all in. You're about to have the time of your life." Her eyes canvassed the living room like she was taking inventory or maybe to check that all was in order. When it appeared to be so, she sauntered in my direction.

Like a game of hide-and-seek, I scrambled down the hall to my bedroom. As I listened with my ear against the door, I could hear her rattling around in the kitchen, opening drawers and pantries. When those sounds ceased, I stuck my head around the door for a quick peek, but could not tell what she was doing. I crouched behind the small table in the hall and watched as Momma emerged with a wooden spoon and an aluminum dishpan we kept underneath the kitchen sink.

Beating the dishpan with the wooden spoon, Momma marched in midnight-sleep regalia down the hall, apparently to awaken the troops for the rally. I could not help but giggle as I watched her. With high-stepping self-assurance, Momma marched, pounded and sang her way down the hall and into the living room, where she continued on her mission marching all around the room. Banging and beating her metal drum in time with the tune, Momma sang as loud as her soft voice would carry. "'Mine eyes have seen the glory of the coming of the Lord; He is trampling out the vintage where the grapes of wrath are stored; He hath loos'd the fateful lightning of his terrible swift sword; His truth is marching on. Glory, glory, hallelujah! Glory, glory, hallelujah! Glory, glory, hallelujah! His truth is marching on.'"

Some minutes later, a cranky Ivylee appeared next to me as I stood in the doorway, and we both watched in either disbelief, or in my case, mock disbelief, as our Momma marched and banged her aluminum drum like an unruly, undisciplined child on a sugar high.

As though incidental to this madness, Momma declared, "Oh, you're awake. Good."

"Either that or dead," I declared.

"'Good'?" Ivylee repeated. "Momma, do you know what time it is? This is not 'good,' Momma."

"Are you okay, Momma?"

"We're the ones that are not okay." Ivylee explained to me. "We're supposed to be asleep."

"What if she's had a stroke, Ivylee?"

"Stroke nothing! You don't act like that when you have a stroke. You fall down on the floor and shake and quiver or something. The only people who act like that are either drunk or crazy. Come over here, Momma, and let me smell your breath."

Indignant at the suggestion, Momma dismissed Ivylee with a wave of her hand. "I will do no such thing. I am perfectly all right. As a matter of fact, I am better than all right. I am jubilant. I'm rejoicing. I'm. . ." Momma paused as she considered what she was. Obviously pleased with herself, she added, "I'm ready. Now help me prepare the living room. We're about to have a service."

Ivylee and I looked at each other in drop-faced amazement. Even I, who had been somewhat prepped for this with my eavesdropping, was not prepared for another full-blown service. I assumed and hoped we would get an announcement that the services had come to an end. Then it occurred to me that although Bunk may have returned, his return might be nothing more than an extension of Momma's madness. The thought sent outraged shock waves through me, and I was instantly on alert.

"A service!" Ivylee squealed.

"We just had a service a few hours ago, Momma."

"Come here and let me smell your breath." Ivylee moved in Momma's direction, and Momma moved away. "Now stand still. This is for your own good. And you better pray I smell something or it's the cracker factory for you. Right, Sister?"

"Will you please leave me alone?"

Ivylee grabbed Momma by her shoulders and sniffed.

"I have not been drinking. You know very well that I don't drink, except in the wintertime when I get a cough, and then I have a smidgen of Muscatel."

"With the way you've been behaving recently, Momma, a person could easily believe wintertime for you was an ongoing season."

"Breathe for me," Ivylee insisted.

"I will not."

Ignoring Momma, Ivylee sniffed Momma's breath. "Smells all right to me. Maybe a whiff of onion left over from supper. Did you forget to brush your teeth, Momma?"

As I considered yet another service, I could feel my shoulders sliding into a slump as the possibility of the continuation of the last nine years of our lives loomed before me. "You're starting to act like Precious, Momma, and that's not something to be proud of."

"Oh, but you're wrong."

Tired and defeated, I flopped down onto the overstuffed chair as I pondered what I was going to do with the three of them. "Precious is peculiar, Momma. Do you want to be peculiar?"

"Maybe you should sit down, Momma. I know I should." Ivylee sat on the sofa, pulled her knees to her chest and her gown down over her buckled legs to keep them warm. As she looked about the sofa, she asked, "Where's the African?"

"It's an afghan, Ivylee. You don't pull an African over you. An African is a person from Africa. How many times do I have to tell you that? But then with your loose morals, pulling an African over you might be accurate."

"Do you want me to participate in this conversation, Sister? Or do you just want to have it by yourself?"

"By myself."

"Now girls. We don't have time to argue. We have to

192

get ready. This is going to be the best one yet."

Like a corkscrew, Ivylee twisted back and forth on the sofa to keep her legs warm inside her gown. When she bounced up enough to pull her gown down further, Bunk's leg rolled into her. "What is this thing doing here? You been playing dress-up again, Momma?"

Had I not been so agitated from lack of sleep and the idea of yet another service, I think I would have giggled. As it was, I was no longer in the mood to be jovial and too tired to even enjoy persecuting Ivylee. "It's the wee hours of the morning, Momma. I have to get up in a few hours to feed the chickens. So please, can we. . ."

Disgusted, Ivylee popped up like she was being called to the front of the class and stomped across the floor to the screen door. "Momma, I want you to look out there. See, it's pitch-dark, except for that light over near the barn. Dark is when people sleep. It's not daylight at all out there. The chickens aren't even up yet, Momma. Sister can't feed sleeping chickens. They might not remember they been fed, and then she'd have to do it all over again." Ivylee paused as she considered what she had said. "Why is there a light near the barn?"

As pleased as a sheep dog at rounding a straggler, Momma answered in a tone that suggested this was yesterday's news, "Oh, don't worry. It's just Bunk."

"*Just* Bunk?" Ivylee bellowed.

"After all these years, its 'just Bunk?'" I asked.

"Yes, isn't it wonderful?" Momma marveled. "And he says he's going to help me find God."

That did it for me. I may as well have been a firecracker and Momma's words the match. Nine years of living this lunacy could not easily be swept away, and the image of the three of them leading evangelical parades while I, their personal clown, ran behind with scoop and shovel, was a bit more than I could handle at this hour. "Help you find God!"

As I considered the possibilities this image called to mind, the excitement of my previous anticipation evaporated. Frustration rose in me like hot lava in a volcano, and I could feel a tirade coming on in spite of myself. I had played this game for so long, I was no longer certain of the two of them, as well as Bunk's sudden, miraculous recovery, and I was not ready to be disappointed again. "Bunk is lost himself. He can't help you find God. He probably couldn't find the sun when it comes up. That does it. I'm leaving. You have gone too far, Momma. And this time, there's no stopping me. There is no way in tarnations that I'm going to stay here and mind eighteen thousand cackling chickens, a sex-starved, half-wit sister, a mother whose life is more make believe than real, and a family pet, who is literally a member of the family, and who has obviously, through some further act of insanity, become an evangelist. That's going too far, Momma!"

"I am not a half-wit."

In spite of my fatigue, like a roman candle, my frustration flared, and the balls of fire sent me stomping back and forth across the living room, as if my actions could stomp out whatever further craziness was coming forth from people I once thought were my parents. "And just where did Bunk find God? Out in the yard digging doodle bug holes in the dirt?"

"I didn't know you could find God there. No wonder He was lost."

I glared at Ivylee with such daring in my eyes that the glare could have probably perforated her ears.

With her hands together as if to say a blessing and in a cheerful voice that suggested she had been cut loose from her anchor, Momma replied, "It doesn't matter where he found Him as long as he found Him, right?"

"That's right, Sister," Ivylee agreed. "It doesn't matter. Now let's go back to bed. We can all rest better knowing that Bunk found God. I know I can."

"No. We've got some important business to take care of, so we can't go back to bed now." As if our protests were non-existent, Momma scampered over to the sideboard and removed a lace tablecloth from inside a drawer.

"Momma, there is nothing in our lives important enough to get up in the middle of the night."

"Now don't be like that, Sister. I want you to have a good time." Momma folded the lace tablecloth in the shape of a triangle and draped it across her shoulders. "How does this look?"

"If you were mahogany and had four legs, it would look great."

"It looks lovely, Momma, just like a bride. Now can we go back to bed?"

A look of surprised remembrance crossed Momma's brow. "A bride. I wonder whatever happened to Meter Reader."

"Meter Reader was really real?" Ivylee asked with equal surprise.

"Oh, yes, he was real, wasn't he, Sister?"

"I'm not sure anymore. I've begun to believe nothing is real, except maybe the reality of what isn't. And I'm not at all sure that makes any sense, but I'm too tired to consider it further."

Momma continued her exploration of the sideboard's contents. "Oh, well, we can't wait for him. We got things to do. Ivylee, Honey, run and get me some bobby pins, please."

"What for? You gonna roll your hair at this hour?"

"You'll see. Now hurry up."

In her usual whiney voice, Ivylee begrudgingly agreed. "Oh, all right, but I don't know why I always have to be the one to run errands. I'm not the errand person. I'm a poet. Poets should be given more consideration." She left the living room and could be heard muttering all the way down the hall.

"Hurry, Honey, and I'll have a little surprise for you when you get back." Momma was examining a lavender doily she had removed from the sideboard. Her face glowed with excitement as she considered the doily. From the funeral flowers, she removed several of the less wilted ones, crossed the room to the sofa, where she draped the lavender doily about Bunk's leg, and arranged the flowers. "Here, you can be the flower boy," she explained as she stuffed the wilted funeral flowers into the overalls surrounding the leg.

Bunk's dead, amputated leg had just been elevated to flower boy. At this point, I felt I could no longer show surprise at anything Momma did. Had she landed on the roof in a fuzzy red suit surrounded by tiny reindeer and shouting "Ho-Ho-Ho," it would not have aroused or registered the slightest sliver of amazement in me. I had begun to wonder how in my brief existence on this earth I had offended my creator so severely.

"Please try to be reasonable, Momma," I begged. "Life is difficult here at best."

"I know, Honey, and that's why we have to fix it."

From the sideboard, she removed linen napkins that were edged with the same lace as that of the tablecloth and unfolded them with a shake of her hand.

The errand girl returned carrying a handful of bobby pins and flounced into the living room like a chicken from its roost. "Here, Momma, I brought a dozen. I hope that's enough."

"That should do it. Now sit down, Sweetheart, and let

me pin your veil."

Like the little robot Ivylee was for Momma, she sat on the arm of the sofa while Momma pinned one of the lace napkins to her hair.

"Are we gonna have a wedding, Momma? Who's getting married? Is it me?"

"Sister, come here, and let me do yours."

"Momma, please. Don't make me sit through one of these services with a napkin pinned to my head." I stood with the intention of leaving the room.

"Oh, it'll be fun. Now come on."

When I did not move, Momma came and pushed me into a sitting position on the opposite end of the sofa. "It has to stop somewhere, Momma."

"Must you always be an ole poop, Sister? You're never going to have any fun in life if you don't start looking at the bright side." Momma pinned the napkin to my hair and stood back to evaluate her work.

"I'm afraid this *is* the bright side."

"That's nice, dear, but there's no need to be afraid." Turning her head from side-to-side like a cuckoo bird evaluating a moth for a meal, Momma concluded, "That looks lovely, dear."

Ivylee's excitement was beginning to blossom, and she danced around the room in her napkin headdress. "Oh, this is so exciting! Who's getting married, Momma? Is it me?"

"Nobody's getting married, not to anybody new anyway. It's a renewing of vows, as they say."

Ivylee stopped dancing. "We got all dressed up, and all we're gonna do is renew some old vows? I want a wedding. I don't need any old vows."

"Who's to marry, Ivylee? You think Momma's got somebody growing out there in the garden for you?"

"Now come and sit down, Ivylee. Momma's got some

good news for all of us."

Disappointed and pouting, Ivylee slunk across the room and sat on the other arm of the sofa.

"Guess what," Momma teased. "Bunk's back! Bunk's back, and we're going to bury the leg. Isn't that exciting?"

I studied Momma's face intently, as if by doing so I could discern if this was truth or fiction. I was not yet ready to wholeheartedly believe Momma would really go along with burying the leg. "Bunk's really back? And you're sure he's not Precious anymore? And you're going to bury Bunk's leg? You're not just confused or making this up?"

Pleasure lit up Momma's face like a candle and seemed to flicker in her eyes. "Oh, he's precious all right. He's my precious Bunk, and he just came and knocked on my door last night. Isn't that wonderful?"

Years of training left me suspicious of Momma's sense of reality, and I stared at her like a weary parent at wit's end with a wayward child. Again, my anger mounted until I stood and paced back and forth in front of Momma like I didn't know whether to spank her or send her to her room. "All of a sudden, he decides to come in off the funny farm after all these years? We been having a memorial service for his dang leg every day for what seems like an eternity, and now whatta we gonna do? We're going to bury it! Why in blue-blazes are we gonna bury the dang thing if we've been saving it for him all this time?" While I knew that from me, this made no sense at all, especially since I had been encouraging interment for years, I was afraid to believe, and not at all convinced, Momma would indeed bury the leg. And so I tested her, knowing quite well that the best, the only place for a dead leg was a deep hole in the ground.

198

"Says he doesn't need it, and he doesn't appear to need it, except he gets awful confused about whose it is."

Ivylee slid sideways down the arm of the sofa to the seat and propped her feet upon the coffin. "But what are we gonna use for a coffee table?"

Oblivious to Ivylee, and probably to me, Momma stated, "And he's gotten real religious. Says the most pretty things you ever heard."

Overwhelming fear that Momma and Bunk might become holy-rollers and turn the farm and me, the caretaker, into some sort of evangelistic free-for-all sideshow, I dove into a diatribe of disbelief with such intensity as if to extinguish and annihilate any notion before it took hold. "Carn-sarn it, Momma, that does it! I'm not staying, and I'm not kidding either. You can just have me locked up, because enough is enough." Although I threw my hands up in the air, I was not ready to pull them back to my side, and in frustration pulled my hair instead. Momma, through completely illogical reasons, and I do believe unintentional, had found my breaking point, and I began to understand why Bunk may have gone berserk so many years ago. Reasoning with Momma had become as futile as telling an infant not to cry when hungry, and a crying infant would no doubt be easier to endure.

"You're right, Sister. I couldn't agree with you more. I think you should leave, not until after the service of course. But after that, you can leave anytime you want to."

Momma smiled as sweet as sorghum syrup, and I stopped stone-still like someone had disconnected my plug. With an unwavering stare meant to size up the seriousness of her comment, I contemplated my Momma like someone was introducing us for the first time, and then I heard myself say, "Are you for real?"

Momma crossed her heart with childlike promise. "Cross my heart, and hope to, to come alive. How about that?" Again, with the sweet smile, she waited for my reaction.

"You're really going to let me leave? You won't have the sheriff pick me up?" Every suspicion I ever owned came together in this question.

"I only did that three times, Sister."

"And I only ran away three times, Momma."

"Oh, well," Momma flung the back of her hand forward as though to dismiss this piece of information as totally ludicrous. "I won't have you picked up this time, I promise. I only did it before because somebody had to run the farm, and you were the only one who could."

Ivylee's eyes were wide and an element of fear laced the sound of her voice. "What about me? Do I have to go to?"

Before Momma could respond, the screen door opened, and he entered. He said nothing at first, and I could not help but wonder who stood there. Yesterday, he was Precious; a few hours ago, he was Mr. Robinson; and now, according to Momma, he was Bunk. For some strange reason at this moment, I considered his name for the first time, not him, but his name. Why had he been named Bunk? Was he truly bunk? And if so, why? Was it a family name? A childhood nickname that never left? Or one that Momma had given him for some reason known only to the two of them? Who was he? Not anybody I knew, at least not recently.

Momma smiled and blushed like an innocent young girl on her wedding night, and they exchanged looks of recognition that I had not seen between the two of them in a long time. Maybe Bunk *had* come home, but nine years of absence still stoked my suspicion.

"No, Honey, of course not. You can stay for as long as you like. Neither of you ever have to go anywhere, if you don't want to. Right, Bunk?"

Hanging the flashlight on the coat rack, he replied, "That's right, 'for as long as you like.' But I hope you won't continue to waste your time waiting for Mr. Robinson, Ivylee."

Probably for lack of anything else to say and uncertain of the guidelines of this new game, Ivylee puffed herself up like an angry adder and spit out, "I'll have you know my Mr. Robinson is well worth waiting for." With a note of pleading in her voice and her eyes focused on Momma, she asked, "Besides, if I don't wait for Mr. Robinson, who am I going to wait for?"

"We can take care of all that later, Honey. Everything's going to be just fine. You'll see, but right now, we need to get on with the service." Just as a mother straightens her child's bonnet before Easter pictures, Momma adjusted the lace-embroidered napkin pinned to Ivylee's hair. "You look just darling."

"Why, thank you, Momma. I'll pretend I'm practicing for my wedding."

Momma turned to Bunk and with a look of sudden awareness, asked, "Oh, my, should we go put on our mourning dresses?"

"Since we're putting the leg 'to rest,' I think we're all dressed appropriately, except for me. I may be a tad underdressed."

"Well, we can fix that." Momma opened the doors to the front of the sideboard to inventory the remaining contents. "Let's see what we have here. Not much left, I'm afraid. Oh, here's something." Momma removed a silver breadbasket and handed it to Bunk. "Here, put this on."

Like she was the teacher and he the obedient student, Bunk took the breadbasket and placed it on top of his head. "How does this look?"

"You look stunning," Momma assured him.

"Why, thank you, Ma'am. You have made my morning." He paused before whispering, "And you fill my life."

Ivylee and I sneaked glances toward one another like we wondered if we were in the wrong house.

Observing this scene and how it could possibly play to the outside world, I looked about the room to see if perhaps Rod Serling had slipped in unawares to televise it for a segment of "The Twilight Zone."

"'Putting the leg to rest' here at Robin's Rest. What a sweet way to put it." Momma nodded her head in happy affirmation. "Ivylee, would you like to recite one of your poems for this special occasion?"

Caught off guard for probably the first time in her poetically challenged life, Ivylee hesitated. "A poem? Uh, let me think."

While Ivylee thought, which would no doubt take some time since she had never done this before, Momma turned to me and asked, "What about you, Sister? Anything you wanna say?"

"Yes. A-men!"

Momma shared one of those knowing-parent looks with Bunk. "Oh, Sister's getting all spiritual on us, Bunk." Then as if an important task had been overlooked, Momma motioned with the open-palm of her hand for everything to halt, "Oh, wait just a minute." Like a chipmunk gathering chestnuts, she scooted to the sofa and scooped up the leg. Her next scoot placed her in front of me, holding the leg at the end of outstretched arms like it was a megaphone into which I was supposed to address the world. "Here, Sister."

"I don't want that thing, Momma."

"Don't you want to say goodbye to it?"

Exasperated beyond my normal threshold, I rolled my

eyes while Momma again stood firm, waiting for her obstinate child to do the right thing. Through clinched teeth, I finally muttered, "Goodbye."

"Is that all you got to say to it after all these years? After all its meant to you?"

From what felt like endless past experience, I recognized that I would either cooperate or we would be standing there until the end of time. And so I forced myself to speak with about as much emotion as reciting the entire "Constitution of the United States" to a class of dodge ball players in grade school ready to go outside for recess. "What its meant to me, I could not express in a few words. Okay?"

"How sweet. Sister, you constantly amaze me. Isn't that right, Bunk? Isn't our Sister amazing?"

Bunk smiled; I smiled; and Momma continued. "Would you like to say something else? Can be anything you like. This *is* a special occasion."

"Okay," I said in resignation. "There was this one thing I never got to recite in school. How about it I recite it now? 'Out, out brief candle. . .'"

"Oh, the candles," Momma recalled aloud as she pushed the leg into my arms. Again, like a chipmunk on a nut-finding expedition, Momma scurried to the sideboard.

While Momma plowed through the drawer in search of candles, there was a sudden, loud knock at the door. Considering the hour, the knock startled all of us. The fear in Momma's eyes surfaced in the sound of her voice, as she cried, "Bunk?"

As he moved to Momma's side and placed his arm around her, girded in calmness, Bunk's voice soothed Momma. "It's okay." Whoever was at the door or whatever had alarmed Momma, Bunk's demeanor suggested his intention to eliminate it.

I'm not sure which surprised me more, the knock at the door or Bunk's reaction to Momma. Maybe Bunk really was back.

Chapter **17**

The Homecoming

The knock on the door had taken all of us by surprise, and the three of them locked their eyes on me as if I were the watchman. The question in everyone's eyes was "who calls at dawn," and the ultimate answer was "only a harbinger of bad news." And here we were at this hour in our nightgowns with napkins pinned to our hair for a "let's pretend" wedding coupled with a mock funeral for an amputated leg. "Could any bad-news-bird out do this," I wondered, as I placed the leg on the sofa to attend the knock. Flashing through my mind was the possibility, although remote, that on the other side of the door was a reporter from one of the magazines Ivylee enjoys, and that tomorrow we would see ourselves in shocking front cover photographs shared across the country.

"It's Meter Reader," I announced with relief as I held the door open.

"Howdy, folks."

"Oh, Meter Reader," Momma greeted. "How nice of you to join us. We were beginning to think you weren't real. Did we send you an invitation?"

"Well, Ma'am, you gave me an invite to marry your Ivylee, and I been studying on it, and I thought. . ." Just at that moment, Meter Reader's eyes fell on the open coffin on top of the sideboard. "You're not burying her, are you?"

"Oh, no, Meter Reader. We only bury the dead around here. Seems to work better that way." As proud as a peacock with tail feathers up and open in fan-like regalia, Momma exclaimed, "We're having a sunrise service."

"Well, light my candle." Meter Reader hollered. "Last time I was at a sunrise service,. . ."

While Meter Reader contemplated his response, Ivylee moved to Momma's side, bumping her shoulder against Momma's back and looking all the while like she could devour a whole birthday cake by herself. Standing slightly behind Momma, Ivylee twisted and turned in cow-eyed anticipation.

"Goodness me," Momma declared. "Where are my manners? Everybody, this is Meter Reader. And Meter Reader, this is Ivylee." Ivylee peeked around Momma looking like a hungry harlot trying to overcome an attack of shyness. "Meter Reader was here earlier looking for power. Did you find your power, Son? Bunk found his." Momma giggled, her eyes twinkling in Bunk's direction.

"Well, Ma'am, let me tell you, I was out in your yard trying to find your meter when I got this call on my Walkie-Talkie, and they said I had gotten a phone call from over at the mortuary. So I went to return the call and when I did, them morticians said somebody had accidentally made themselves a burger outta my Barbara, and I best come get her before she was all eaten up. So that's what I did."

This amazed even Momma, whose mind most often

seemed more capable of processing this type of information. For several minutes, she did not appear to be able to react and even then stuttered before she could get her mouth situated as to what she was going to say next. "Barb. . . Barbara is his poor, departed wife that got chewed up by a truck."

"A truck." Bunk repeated in a hoarse-sounding voice.

"A truck that chews up trees and limbs," I explained. "She was sitting on a tree limb, and apparently the County workers didn't see her when they were trimming back the trees and accidentally dropped her into that big wood chipper of theirs." Bunk looked like I might have told him that Momma had joined a cult, and they were looking for one-legged people to sacrifice to the Ouija board god.

"That's right," Meter Reader confirmed. "And they couldn't hear her either because some Blue Angels were flying over."

Incredulous, Bunk looked first at Meter Reader and then at me in what appeared to be an effort to wrap his mind around this image. Unfortunately, at this point, I had resigned myself to whatever lay ahead, no matter how bizarre, and so in response, I simply smiled and shrugged my shoulders like he might have asked me if it was going to rain.

"Oh," Bunk responded in kind.

"Anyways," Meter Reader continued, "I went over to the mortuary and picked up my Barbara and took her home, but I couldn't rest a bit, knowing she was sitting out there in my refrigerator, so I got up to take her for a ride, hoping like heck that I could figure out a place to put her. And that's when I spotted your light on and thought I'd drop in for a visit, and maybe marry your Ivylee, that is, if'en she'll have me. Of course, I got to figure out what to do with this old wife first, I reckon."

"I'll have you." Ivylee answered quicker than a roach bug running across the floor. As she stepped from behind Momma and toward Meter Reader, she added, "I don't have anybody either, except for Mr. Robinson, and I have begun to believe that he has not been truthful with me."

As difficult as it was, I did not say a word.

"Oh, my," Meter Reader muttered.

"Couldn't you just put her in the graveyard?" I asked. "That's where most people put them."

"I tried, but she was so mean don't nobody want their kin laying next to her. Guess I'm gonna have to bury her down in my cow pasture, but I didn't know if the cows wouldn't try to dig her up too. They didn't like her none either. She used to spit on them. That woman could spit further than anybody I ever saw."

Bunk made a guttural sound in his throat, before speaking. "Momma, maybe we could help Meter Reader out." With his head, he motioned toward the coffin.

"Oh. Oh?" Momma acknowledged, looking in the direction of the coffin. "Yes, yes we could. Meter Reader, we're about to have a service for Bunk's leg, and we could include your Barbara. You could stick her right in there with Bunk's leg. I don't think it would mind at all. Probably appreciate the company."

"Where is your Barbara?" Ivylee asked moving ever closer to Meter Reader.

"Actually, she wasn't mine. Barbara was the type that don't belong to nobody except herself."

"But she was your wife, wasn't she?" Ivylee stood at Meter Reader's side.

"No, I was her husband, but I don't reckon she was ever my wife, 'cept for now. She's sorta mine now since nobody else wants her. And I guess that's why I don't know what to do with her. I ain't never had her before."

"Oh," Momma sympathized. "Well, you can have Ivylee here."

"Yeah, Ivylee likes being had," I added. "Be like virgin territory, and that's about the only thing about her that is."

With her hand on her hip and her words aimed in my direction, Ivylee declared, "I'll have you know I've been a virgin many times." Turning toward Meter Reader, Ivylee assured him. "And don't you worry none either. I can pretend real good."

Apparently, Ivylee lit Meter Reader's candle. "Wow-wee! I can tell already that I'm gonna like you a lot!" Meter Reader appeared tickled all the way down to his toes.

"I know," Momma declared. "We can have a funeral and a wedding. Be like one big, happy party, and it'll save on refreshments too." Momma looked to Bunk for approval, and he nodded in agreement and would have probably done so no matter what off-the-wall suggestion Momma made. I was just grateful she didn't want to hold all these ceremonies at the Community Center.

Momma removed the lace tablecloth from her shoulders and draped it around Ivylee. "Oh, you look like a bride. I think I'm going to cry."

"Do I really, Momma? Oh, I always wanted to." Ivylee twisted and turned back and forth like she was in a swivel chair trying to locate its range. "But I don't have a bridal bouquet."

Ivylee had always served as a source of inspiration for Momma's creative endeavors, and Momma had never disappointed her. Her eyes scoured the room until they fell upon the flowers poked into the overalls on Bunk's leg. Her face lit up like a firefly when she spotted the lavender doily. Momma grasped the doily, snatched three of the artificial doves hanging from the ceiling and arranged them in the center of the doily. As odd as it was, it looked rather sweet and appropriate. "Here, Ivylee, pretend these are peonies."

Ivylee grabbed the doily and dove arrangement like Momma had granted her greatest wish. "Oh, thank you. You always make everything all right." With tears in her eyes, Ivylee hugged Momma.

While I observed the two of them in what would appear to be their permanent out-to-lunch manner and in some unexplainable way, found it warm to watch, I wondered if I, like the "Wicked Witch of the West," might not be melting.

With his head down, Meter Reader cast his eyes toward Ivylee. "You do look mighty fine."

Wiggling like she had bugs in her britches, Ivylee snuggled in closer to Meter Reader. "You think so?" Flirt that she was, Ivylee tilted that empty head of hers to one side, batted her eyelashes, and slid her hand inside Meter Reader's arm. Scarlet had nothing on Ivylee. "How do you feel about muffins?"

"I like muffins. Usually have them with butter."

"Oooh, that does sound like fun."

"Ivylee," I cautioned, fearful of what could come next.

"Aren't they a darling couple?" Momma sighed. "And Sister here can be the matron of honor."

"Maid, Momma, maid."

"Oh, that's right. We don't have anybody for Sister. You got anybody else out in your truck, Meter Reader?"

"Just my dog and my bag of Barbara."

"Well, we can't marry Sister to a dog. Wouldn't look right."

"Thank you, Momma."

"Maybe Sister would like to go back to school," Bunk suggested.

"Would you like to do that, Sister? Me and Bunk could

210

probably manage if you would. Don't you think we could, Bunk?"

"Yes, between the two of us, I think we could."

"Well, gee, I don't know. I've never. . . I'll have to think about it. It's been a long time. Could we talk about it later?"

"In your own time, Sister," Momma reassured.

Bunk moved next to Momma, who flashed him a grin that belonged to him alone. "We need to get on with it. Sun will be up soon, and there'll go our sunrise service."

"Bunk's right. Meter Reader, you best go get your wife outta your truck." Like making a bed, Momma smoothed the satin lining of the coffin. "You can roll her up and stick her in right here. Bunk's leg has gone kinda soft from being out of the freezer all this time, so there should be plenty of room."

"If'en you're sure, Ma'am. I sure wouldn't want to impose."

"Aren't you a sweetheart? Why, no, it's no imposition at all. Now you scoot on out to your truck and get your wife."

"Yes, Ma'am." Meter Reader patted Ivylee's hand before he moved away from her and out the door, and Ivylee sighed and twirled like a spinning top slowing down.

Momma canvassed the room to take stock. "Let's see. What else do we need? Matches." While Momma looked for matches in the sideboard, Bunk stepped outside the screen door. When he returned, he carried behind his back a garland of flowers he had woven together. With one hand, he gently tugged on Momma's arm until she faced him, and then placed the garland of flowers upon her head.

"Oh, my. How beautiful. And how sweet." Momma looked at Bunk like I hope to look at someone myself someday. "I love you, Bunk."

Bunk flashed his slanted grin and kissed her on the cheek. For the first time in a long time, Ivylee and I exchanged glances and smiles about something on which we could both agree.

"Here, let me help you with those candles." While Momma held the candles from the end tables, Bunk struck a match and lit each one. From the sideboard, Momma removed a three-tiered, Christmas candleholder that was triangular in shape like the gable of a roof. From a drawer, she removed three tapered candles, which Bunk lit and Momma placed into the candleholder.

"Ivylee, you been thinking about what you want to say to Meter Reader in your ceremony?"

With all the depth of a soap dish, Ivylee responded, "Well, yes, Momma, I have. I thought I'd say 'I do.'"

"Don't you think you ought to add a little something to it? I mean after all, Ivylee, you are a poet."

"All right, if you think so, Momma. But you can't rush these things. Being an artist is a gift, and you have to wait till the muse strikes you. Otherwise you don't know what gobble-dee-gook you liable to come up with."

"Did you say muse or mule?"

Ignoring me, Ivylee continued, "And not only that, Momma. Meter Reader might be threatened by my talent and may not want me to be a poet. You never know, and a wife has to consider these things. You should know that, Momma."

"Ivylee, have you ever considered that you might be delusional?" Thank the Almighty that Meter Reader returned at that moment before I barfed all over myself.

With her hand on her hip, Ivylee turned her snooty self toward me and declared, as if this were the answer to every mystery that ever was, "I've got a man."

Carrying a white Styrofoam ice chest, Meter Reader

announced, "Here she is! I'll just roll her out and stick her in there, if you're sure it's okay?"

"You go right ahead, Son. We're trying to move along here before the sun comes up," Bunk reminded.

Meter Reader placed the ice chest on the floor and removed his bag of Barbara while the rest of us watched with drop-faced, rapt attention. It would probably be safe to say that not a one of us had ever witnessed someone roll their bag of wife on the floor like she was a meatloaf being shaped and prepared for baking. When finished, Meter Reader patted each end of the rolled log, as though tapping the final touch.

In what sounded like lack of breath or controlled disbelief, Bunk inquired, "Would you like to say something over her, Meter Reader?"

Still on his knees, Meter Reader held his bag of wife out in front of him. "You would have been a good wife if you hadn't been so bad." Smiling, he gazed up at Momma and Bunk for approval.

"How about if Ivylee says something over her?" Momma suggested. "Ivylee's a poet, you know. And she's good with framing words. I'm sure she could frame you up something real nice. How about it, Ivylee?"

"Yes, I remember you told me that, Ma'am." With a sappy sort of smile, Meter Reader glanced in Ivylee's direction. "I never known a poet before."

"Neither has she," I pointed out, "and could we please get on with this?"

"Meter Reader, why don't you stand over there next to Ivylee? It will give y'all a chance to get to know one another. Ivylee, you got anything you can say about his old wife?" Both Momma's eyes and the tone of her voice appeared to be pleading with Ivylee.

With the plastic bag in his arms, Meter Reader stepped

in front of Ivylee, and as though presenting her as an offering, he held his bag of wife out in front of him. Ivylee turned and handed her bouquet of artificial doves to me before extending her arms to Meter Reader. She smiled as she took his hands in hers to form a bridge between their two bodies. On top of the bridge lay the bag of wife. As though rocking an infant, Ivylee swayed their arms to and fro while she sang, "'Roll, roll, roll your wife gently on the floor, Doodley, Doodley, Doodley, Doo, Ain't your wife no more. Roll, roll, roll your wife just a little more, Swing, Swing, Swing, Swing, Life is but a door.'"

"Ivylee, you are such a wonder, Child." While Momma applauded, Bunk dropped his head to both hide and stifle a chuckle. Although I kept it to myself, I agreed with Momma. I "wondered" at what door Ivylee had checked her brain before entering.

"That was beautiful." Meter Reader marveled as he leaned forward and planted a kiss on Ivylee's cheek.

Ivylee's face lit up, and I considered that she might not make it through the remainder of the service with her clothes on.

Momma cooed to Bunk's leg while cradling it in her arms one last time before placing it inside the coffin. As gently as emptying a pound cake onto a cooling rack, she lowered the leg into its final resting place.

Meter Reader gathered up his bag of Barbara, and Momma helped him squish her inside the coffin beside Bunk's leg. "That's good, Son. Looks like you done this kind of thing before."

"Well, no, not exactly. But I used to make Easter baskets at the five and dime."

"That so? What a coincidence. We used to make rabbits." Momma stepped back to admire Bunk's leg and Meter Reader's bag of wife lying side-by-side inside the coffin. "My, my, they do make a lovely twosome. Don't you think so, Bunk?"

Bunk raised his eyebrows and nodded his head in questionable agreement while Meter Reader made his way back to Ivylee's side.

"Sister, you were saying something about candles?" Momma reminded, as once again she held the Christmas candleholder between her and Bunk.

"Candles? Oh, yeah, let's see. "'. . .Out, out brief candle. Life's but a walking shadow. . .'" For dramatic effect, I blew out the candle on the end table closest to me.

Momma beamed with parental pride. "Why, Sister, that was lovely. Did you write it yourself? Are you going to be a poet now too?"

"No, Momma. Was something I had to memorize in school."

With a twist of her chin as her nose went up in the air, Ivylee declared, "It sounds like something you'd write. Made no sense at all." In an effort to explain to Meter Reader, Ivylee added, "She's always putting on airs she don't have. Pay no mind to her. She thinks she's the queen of the chicken farm."

I had often wondered what I thought, but being "queen of the chicken farm" had never been a conclusion I had ever reached. Before I could respond, Momma asked, "Would you like to say something, Meter Reader?"

"What do you recommend? I've never done this proper."

"Well, I got something I'm gonna say to Bunk. I've been memorizing just for this occasion. You can repeat after me if you like. It's beautiful, and it comes from the Bible."

"Okay, sure, Ma'am. I'll be happy to say anything you want me to. They's just one thing I got to say before we have the ceremony though." Meter Reader let out a sigh like he was about to announce that he was wanted in forty-nine states. "Ivylee, my wife, Barbara, she said nobody deserved me. I just thought I should tell you that."

"But she didn't know Ivylee," I pointed out.

Ivylee pushed herself up next to Meter Reader. "Meter Reader, my Momma always told me I deserved the best, so you must be the best."

"My, you sure are sweet. Let's get on with it."

Probably the most thoughtful wedding gift I could give to Meter Reader was put his name on a number of prayer lists.

"Are we ready now?" Bunk reminded.

Momma motioned for me to switch off the overhead light, which I did, before I wedding-marched back across the room to the center of the ceremonial space. With only the candles providing light, the room took on an ethereal atmosphere. Despite the napkins, tablecloths, and breadbasket, in the flickering of the three Christmas candles, each person looked surprisingly handsome. Holding the Christmas candles between them, Momma gazed into Bunk's eyes, where she no doubt both found and filled her heart's longing.

With Meter Reader's voice serving as a soft echo, Momma and Meter Reader vowed, "'. . .for whither thou goest, I will go; and where thou lodgest, I will lodge: thy people *shall* be my people, and thy God my God: Where thou diest, will I die, and there will I be buried. . . .'" A peace had settled in Momma's eyes, and she glowed from the presence of it.

As soft as evening's shadow, Bunk whispered, "And I do." In the quiet of the moment, he studied Momma's face as though it were a map to a place he had forgotten, and Momma basked in the warmth of it. After passing the candleholder to me, Bunk and Momma embraced.

Tears welled up in my eyes as I watched the two people I loved most in the world find each other. I closed my eyes and whispered, "Amen."

Confused, Ivylee looked at me and then at Momma. "Do you want us to clap, Momma?"

"Ivylee, this is not a Mt. Sinai softball game."

"Does this mean you're going to cut off your leg, Momma?"

"Ivylee!" I shouted. But as I considered some of Momma's previous logic, for reassurance, I asked, "You wouldn't do that, would you, Momma?"

"Of course not. It's just too confusing. Bunk, would you like to do the honors for Ivylee and Meter Reader since we just gave her away?"

"Sure. I'd be happy to." Bunk stood up straight as though he were about to announce the winner of The World Series. "Under the new bylaws of this household, we now pronounce you Meter Reader and Ivylee."

"Hooray," the ninny yelled. "I always wanted to be one of them."

Looking like he might have swallowed one of the artificial doves, Meter Reader asked, "May I kiss the bride?"

Being the subdued, shy creature she is, Ivylee grabbed Meter Reader by the shoulders and pulled his face to hers with such force that the two of them could have been rendered unconscious. The kiss Ivylee laid on Meter Reader gave us pause to wonder if she was going to suck all the oxygen right out of his lungs. When she allowed the poor boy to come up for air, I offered my condolences. "I can't think of a soul who deserves nobody less." With this I blew out the Christmas candles and placed them on the end table.

In unison, the newly connected couple squeaked, "Why,

thank you, Sister."

"Oh, doesn't that just warm your insides," Momma sighed. "Bunk, you have anything you want to say over your dear, detached leg and its sidekick, Barbara?"

"It's on its way to dawn, Momma. We've been up most of the night carrying on over a dead leg, and I have to feed the chickens in a couple of hours, so can we please be done with it and put the thing to rest?"

"Will you try to show a little sensitivity, Sister?" Momma glanced at Bunk as though to apologize.

"Sister's right. The time is nigh to say goodbye," Bunk chimed. He lowered the lid to the coffin and turned to face the group with his head bowed. "For what we are about to put asunder, let us pray. Dear heavenly Father, please accept this in the spirit in which it is offered, for what is dead within us must pass on, and that which is alive, please awaken to new life. Amen."

After each of us murmured amen, Momma added, "That was lovely, Bunk."

Bunk winked at Momma and motioned toward the coffin. "Meter Reader, you want to give me a hand with this?"

"Sure, Dad."

While Bunk and Meter Reader lifted the coffin, Momma and I prepared the way for them to carry it outside.

Momma stood back and watched as though to take it all in. "Isn't it all just precious?"

While I held the door open and the flashlight, the two men carried the coffin onto the porch. Momma followed with a basket of flowers. Near the edge of the porch, Bunk and Meter Reader set the coffin down. While Bunk repositioned himself to better maneuver the steps, Meter Reader studied the tree stump. In the light from the flashlight, Meter Reader spotted the electrical cord to the rooster clock. "Ma'am, did you realize your clock's not plugged in? Oh, and that reminds me. About your meter, Ma'am, well, I looked all over this place for it, and you know what? You ain't got no meter. You ain't got no meter, and you've had power all along."

"You don't say? Ain't that curious?" Momma handed the basket of flowers to Ivylee. "Here, Ivylee, pluck some petals." Ivylee took hold of the handle with one hand and with the other pulled a handful of petals from the wilting flowers.

"Oh, I know," Momma exclaimed as she scampered back inside. Moments later, she returned carrying the paper wings Ivylee had made for her paper angel poem. After contemplating the tree stump, Momma placed the paper wings among the roots of the stump in front of the doorknob and clock. Hung together, the wings formed a paper heart. Like a kid looking through a toy store window, Momma sang, "It's only a paper heart." Gently, she kissed her fingers and placed them on the paper heart. Pleased, she made her way toward Bunk while she sang, "'On the wings of a snow-white dove, He sends His pure, sweet love, A sign from above—On the wings of a dove. . .'"

With Momma standing in front of him, Bunk placed his arms around her shoulders and with his cheek next to hers, the two of them swayed and sang, "'. . .When troubles surround us, When evil comes, The body grows weak, The spirit grows numb. . .'" From his overall pocket, Bunk removed the rock. Placing the palm of her hand underneath his, Momma contemplated the rock. Like a child arranging a secret garden, Momma took the rock and placed it at the base of the paper heart. She turned to face Bunk, who held out his hand to guide her down the steps, as they continued to sing, "'. . .When these things beset us, He doesn't forget us. He sends down His love, On the wings of a dove.'"

From the porch, I watched Bunk and Meter Reader as they lifted the coffin and eased their way down the steps. Momma and Ivylee followed behind as Bunk and Meter Reader maneuvered the yard. As the little troop made their way toward the barn, Ivylee tossed flower petals into the air.

On the horizon just beyond the barn, the sun was coming up. I was about to turn off the flashlight when I spotted Momma's arrangement. Instead, I stood the flashlight on end underneath the tree stump, where its beam cast light in all directions around some of Momma's many "signs."

From the top of the icebox, I removed the bridal bouquet of artificial doves nestled in the lavender doily. Smiling to myself, I tossed the bridal bouquet into the air, where I caught and held it. With bouquet in hand, I followed along.

At the far side of the farm stood the old, gray barn where robins were at rest in Momma's heart, if nowhere else.

The coffin was closed; the door open.

The End

Postfix

"I am the Alpha and Omega, the beginning and the end, the first and the last. . . the bright and morning star."

—Revelations 22:13 and 16

LaVergne, TN USA
25 November 2009
165269LV00002B/2/A